Redefining America

The Battle for Words,
Meaning, and the
Future of a Nation

Matthew R. Borgner

Table of Contents

Author's Note

To my readers: Understand that the various chapters within this book were written over a time period of several years. The subject matter is based largely on events in time, and with time comes inevitable change.

Also note that as we transitioned at the national level from Republican control to Democrat control and now back to Republican control again, we've experienced tremendous change in the political climate both socially and economically. Currently, the change is coming at a furious pace especially for those of us "taking note."

I believe it's important to remind everyone that any book of this nature will have some chapters and relevant content that ages well and other material that does not. It can be no other way. Please keep these thoughts in mind as you read this book.

Introduction

D o you sometimes feel as if you live in a "world" that you no longer understand? Do you ever think, introspectively, that your personal perceptions, beliefs and understanding of society and relevant issues of the day have somehow come to be deemed by many as wrong, backwards, or even as evil? Have you ever struggled to understand how and why this seems to have happened to you and to others that share your deeply rooted values, beliefs, and ideals?

I'm willing to wager that it isn't you that has changed. Part of the disconnect is that it's the very definition and meaning of the terms, phrases, and concepts that we commonly use to understand and communicate with one another in society that have changed. As you may know, a subset of Americans has been consciously working for many years to redefine what were once commonly understood terms and phrases. But why?

What's the purpose of redefining relevant terms so that these terms and concepts hold new meaning? Who's doing it? As you read this book, you'll see that it's being done for a specific purpose and effect. In this book, we'll delve into the purpose of redefining terms and the effect on America

Words mean things. Words must have specific meaning for individuals and society to share thoughts and develop understanding among one another. If a person refers to the tallest man in the crowd, for example, those within his or her company can determine with some specificity to whom he or she refers.

A shared language is a basic and necessary construct within society. It's inherent within a shared language that words mean the same thing to those fluent in any given language (slang not withstanding). That's the purpose and the essence of having a shared language.

What happens when a group or groups of people take it upon themselves to change shared language to make words or terminology mean something different? Now, think about what would happen if or when these groups of people use nuanced changes to commonly understood words in an effort to make positive or neutral constructs into negative or contentious ones. What happens when these redefined terms are then used to deliberately confuse or change the once universally understood meaning of relevant concepts within society?

Finally, what if these groups of people that work to redefine terms and concepts can successfully weaponize this new language to promote an agenda? What if they could find success in taking concepts that are (or were) universally positive such as "patriotism" and "law abiding" and turning them into something sinister? They could then easily label those that promote such concepts as wrong or even as evil.

The political left in America has been (for many years) selectively redefining terms, phrases and concepts in an effort to push America towards their world view. As is typically the case, they don't do this by clarifying and unifying Americans around their agenda.

Rarely does the American left work in any clear and honest way to win the hearts and minds of Americans. Rather, they've been actively and covertly redefining terms and concepts to do the exact opposite. The political strategy of redefining America is being done to confuse, divide and conquer America to drive a far-left agenda.

In the following chapters we'll look at examples of terms, phrases and concepts that have been redefined by the American left and weaponized against many Americans—perhaps even you.

We'll look at the "old" or once commonly understood definitions. We'll break down the American left's newly fabricated ones. And we'll look at the effect of this political strategy on America. We'll even associate a few names when and where proper "credit" is due.

Now, on to our first chapter.

1

Truth

As I write this chapter, America is as divided now as it has been since perhaps the 1960s. This is due in large part to now having two (or more) versions of so-called "truth." How has this happened?

Over recent years, something has changed regarding the term or concept of truth. Dictionary.com defines truth as:

> 1. The true or actual state of a matter, 2. Conformity with fact or reality, 3. A verified or indisputable fact, proposition, principle, or the like, 4. The state or character of being true. 5. Actuality or actual existence. 6. An obvious or accepted fact; truism.

The overarching crux of the meaning is that truth is a matter of fact. Truth is factually based. Truth is, therefore, inarguable, as no argument can refute matters of fact. They simply are as they are. Period. This is the universally understood meaning of the word or concept of truth. Or is it?

Interestingly, truth is defined by Merriam-Webster as including within its definition, "Sincerity in action, character, and utterance." How does this qualification differ from the others? In a word, greatly. This is new, at least in a sense, in that it doesn't fit the same universally understood meaning that requires truth to be rooted in fact. It's a definition that only requires one to sincerely believe in something to deem it to be the truth.

It takes the concept or the meaning of truth from a matter of fact to a matter of sincere belief. Get it? Under this definition or qualification of truth, if you sincerely believe that something represents truth, then it simply does, whether it meets the standard of being factual or not.

Can truth, then, stand in opposition to relevant facts and even to reality? Under this definition, yes it can. Under this definition, the concept of truth does not need to match reality at all.

Have you ever heard anyone utter the phrase, that's "my truth?" What a loaded phrase and concept! I recall first hearing someone introduce that abstraction into a heated debate over some social issue being discussed. It's a "showstopper," so to speak. And it's meant to be just that.

What does the phrase, "my truth" mean? You may find it interesting that neither Merriam-Webster nor Dictionary. com recognized the phrase upon my research. I had to go elsewhere for a definition and found one from the folks at Urbandictionary.com. They did more than attempt to define the phrase. They qualified it with what could be considered "their truth."

According to Urbandictionary.com, "my truth" means:

> Pretentious substitute for "non-negotiable personal opinion." Often used by academics, this is a convenient phrase for avoiding arguments because people can contradict your opinion but not your "truth." The phrase is often used when seeking to justify a controversial personal stance or action because people are not allowed to argue with "your truth."

It draws a parallel and equally weighs conclusions based on emotions or beliefs with those based in fact. In essence, it gives credence to someone's emotionally drawn opinions as if they're more-so. Again, it's an attempt to dishonestly sell or give credence to one's opinion as a matter of indisputable fact.

This leads to questions related to understanding from where this redefinition emanated. Who has been busy promoting to us this new definition of truth? I found an article from the *Philadelphia Inquirer* discussing this matter and who's on record selling this new narrative. In an article written by Anna Orso, from January 10, 2018, titled: "Oprah Says, 'Speak Your Truth.' But How Is That Different From 'The Truth?,'" we begin to identify some advocates. According to the article:

> ...what resonated the most was Winfrey's message of "speaking your truth." The media mogul referenced this three times while addressing the seismic #MeToo movement, including: "What I know for sure is that speaking your truth is the most powerful tool we all have."

Another quote from the same piece reads:

> A conversation has since emerged about whether living out your truth is a slip farther into postmodernism, in which facts are distorted by personal bias. Is living your truth a laudable goal, or is it the left's version of Orwellian doublespeak, similar to "fake news" or "alternative facts?" And what if "your truth" is that the Earth is flat or that dinosaurs helped build the pyramids?

Let's delve into those quotes as they relate to our subject matter. According to the *Philadelphia Inquirer* article, this example of the redefinition of truth came from

Oprah Winfrey as she addressed members of the "Me Too" movement. It was also described as, "the left's version of Orwellian doublespeak." In other words, and to no surprise, according to the *Philadelphia Inquirer*, we can align this narrative to the political left in America.

Don't forget, the Urban Dictionary associated academia as well. This is important because, as the *Philadelphia Inquirer* article also noted, we have a school of thought called postmodernism that's being used by some as the philosophical underpinning in challenging the concept of truth.

In short, much like the concepts of moral or cognitive relativism, some on the left also believe that truth is relative to one's experiences and beliefs versus a matter of being factual. What's noteworthy is that this school of thought came to us through academia and has recently been usurped by the rest of the political left to promote their agenda(s).

Here's a little snippet from a blog called Philosophy Talk, pulled from an article written by Joshua Landy in 2019, titled "Postmodernism: The Decline of Truth":

> The best argument for postmodernism, it seems to me, is that it sought to undermine the hegemony, in the intellectual world, of the white, male, heterosexual, Western standpoint.

What are we learning? There's a political movement in America that's working to redefine the conceptual definition of truth. This is not to say that one party has cornered the market on telling the truth versus the other. Don't misunderstand the point of this chapter or of this book in general. It's not a matter of counting what might constitute a lie coming from the representatives of one political side versus the other. Nor is this about who is guilty of what specific lies. As important as that is, it isn't the focus of this book. This is much larger and deeper in scope.

Our focal point is the redefining of what constitutes the

meaning of terms such as truth. It's about who's actively and knowingly working to change the meaning of such terms or concepts and for what purposes.

The redefining of terms and concepts is being done by the political left to affect change. The American left has taken a page from left-wing academics arguing against what they consider to be White, male, heterosexual, Western viewpoints. They're working to deconstruct American culture to "rid us" of this foundation. They're doing this in part by changing the very definition and concept of truth in this case, to make it relative versus factual. This, in turn, allows them to argue their feelings and beliefs as an equivalent to facts and reality.

All of this is ultimately done to control the political narrative and sell their far-left ideology. It's inherently dishonest. Arbitrary feelings and beliefs don't equate to facts and evidence. Every clear-thinking person knows that. Selling your opinions as fact-based reality is done to shut down opposition and thwart an honest debate. As mentioned earlier, that's a far cry from winning the hearts and minds of others based on the merits of the debate. As a matter of fact, it's quite the opposite.

2

Race and Racism

I cannot think of a more heated and timelier subject for discussion than the concept of race. It just may be the single most prominent focal point of political and social division in America at this snapshot in time. That is a very sad commentary and it's so unnecessary. Over recent years, the subject of race has been increasingly weaponized against America collectively and has been tearing at our fabric like no other issue.

Why? Let's begin this discussion by defining our relevant terms. I'm going to take a few excerpts from my earlier book, *The Freedom Prescription*, to not only define and discuss the concept of race, but to differentiate it from the concept with which it's typically conflated. Allow me to explain.

According to Merriam-Webster, race is defined as "any one of the groups that humans are often divided into based on physical traits regarded as common among people of shared ancestry." The key phrase to understand here is that race is based on physical traits, such as skin color.

This seems simple enough to understand, doesn't it?

That's the beauty of the true and once universally recognized definition of race. As a concept, it's simple. A person's race is or was a set of physical traits, a physical construct. How and why has that changed?

America's understanding of race has become so much more than physical differences. It would be impossible to go beyond simply scratching the surface to try to encapsulate in its entirety what constitutes race in 21st Century America in one short chapter. That's because America's understanding of the concept of race has been so successfully manipulated and redefined. The "new" definition of race has also encapsulated within its original definition the concept of culture.

As I wrote in *The Freedom Prescription*:

> It's important to first delve into something that Americans desperately need to properly discern. There's a world of difference between the concepts of race and culture. Twenty-first century America seems to conflate these two very different terms. For some reason, most Americans seem to attribute cultural differences to race. Actually, it's even worse than that. An astounding number of Americans misconstrue the term race while they describe and discuss culture.

I went on to define and discuss the concept of culture:

> The same folks (Merriam-Webster) define culture as "the integrated pattern of human knowledge, belief, and behavior that depends upon the capacity for learning and transmitting knowledge to succeeding generations."
>
> Pay attention here. This is key to understanding the issue. As everyone can see, culture is not physical. It's behavioral, and it's based on knowledge and beliefs passed down from one generation to the next.
>
> Do you see the difference? I contend that America, by and large, does not. It's a problem. It's a very big problem and it's one of a number of reasons why our

nation can't get past our racial strife. How are we supposed to make progress when we lack the basic understanding to differentiate between physical traits and learned behavior?

I know, there's a lot there. The original and true definition of race equates to physical differences only. The new 21st Century definition takes the original definition and adds cultural differences as well. This leads to two pertinent questions: What has been the effect of redefining the concept of race on American society? And why was it done?

When the concept of race was redefined to include and conflate the concept of culture, we saw a real "game changer," so to speak. Remember that *culture is behavioral*. It's learned behavior that has been passed down from one generation to the next. Behavior can be good, bad, or neither.

Unlike so many physical traits, behavior can be positive or negative. It can be harmful or helpful. It can be legal or illegal, etc. Generally speaking, good behavior will typically lead one to a better stake in life while bad behavior will typically lead to a poorer result. That's because behavior involves choice. Here's the bullet point: *The new definition of race now (falsely) involves and includes choices and behavior.*

How has this changed the dynamic regarding race relations in 21st Century America? As the concept of race has been redefined, so too has the concept of racism. Whereas racism was once defined as intolerance towards people due to physical differences, it's now considered to be racist should one disagree with the choices and the behavior of others. This is a monumental paradigm shift in conceptional thought and understanding regarding race in America. And this has undoubtedly led to a more fractured and polarized society.

Under the new definition of racism, one can be successfully labeled as racist for criticizing the *behavior* of people of a different race. For example, if a White person, such as myself, were to criticize the diet of a person of color for including too much fried food rather than a healthier alternative, I would risk being labeled as a racist.

The fact that one's diet has nothing to do with the physical trait of skin color does not matter to anyone that chooses to ascribe to the new definition of racism. Under the new definition, people have "carte-blanche" to ascribe that label to anyone that disagrees with their viewpoint. This is true even if the so-called "racist" comment is a matter of demonstrable fact. *None of that matters.* If it's within someone's culture to commonly choose to fry their food, suggesting replacing some fried meals with some salads for better overall health can and is construed by some people as the practice of racism.

OK, I admit it, that example is a bit frivolous. Besides, it's against my nature to act as the "food police." But you get the point. What's happened in America is that pointing to someone's bad behavior as either a harbinger of bad things or as a reason that led to unfortunate circumstances is now often labeled as racist by others in society. That's what's being experienced by many people across America today. That's the effect of redefining race and racism in the manner it's been done. And, consequently, that's how the concept of racism has been weaponized to pit Americans against one another.

Here's where it gets serious. Now, as a society, we've taken this racism matter to a whole new level. We've gone from using the redefined definition of racism to demonize and shut down dissent and debate over trivial matters (food and diet), personal or otherwise, to now using it to defend behavior that should be universally condemned.

No longer can one point to even overwhelmingly bad behavior such as physically and/or verbally attacking a police officer or dealing drugs or violently rioting in the streets and criticize such behavior without the possible and perhaps likely invocation of racism. As a matter of fact, depending upon one's political affiliation, we can now even predict or assume that a charge of racism will be directed their way. And it can be expected to come from the usual suspects: the political left.

Likewise, we've experienced countless examples of so-called racist attacks for criticism of groups of people that have absolutely nothing to do with any particular race, whatsoever. For example, President Trump was roundly and habitually labeled as racist for his fervent criticisms of the Chinese communist government as he openly blamed "China" countless times publicly for their (mis)handling of the COVID-19 pandemic.

No matter how many times President Trump explained and clarified his convictions, the political left continued to cry, "Racism." The more he indicted China or the Chinese, the louder the cries of "racist" and "racism" grew from the Democrats and partisans on the political left.

This continued despite the fact that *China is not a race, nor is Chinese.* China is a nation. The Chinese are the people of China. Not only did those pertinent facts not concern the American left, they universally ignored President Trump's countless clarifications. None of that mattered. Truth itself didn't matter. The only thing that mattered was "getting Trump" politically using any means available.

Therefore, the American left redefined racism to include criticism of the government and/or governmental policies of China. Criticizing one of our greatest global adversaries was precisely what Trump was doing through the "catcalls" of racism. That and explaining (to no avail) that race had no part in the matter.

Feeling obligated to cite at least one example of the effect of the "racist Chinese Virus" narrative, I'll highlight a piece from North Carolina State University's Office for Institutional Equity and Diversity. In a piece titled: "'Chinese' Virus is a Racist Take—Here's Why," from April 3, 2020, author Mina Ouanvilay wrote the following:

> The 'Chinese' virus remark by Donald Trump in a press conference in March brewed increasing amounts of racism and hate crime in America. By saying Chinese virus, he points fingers specifically at Asian-appearing

people.

She went on to place blame on President Trump for cultivating an environment that resulted in race-based attacks both verbally and physically, around the nation.

Now, let's review the facts of the Chinese Virus narrative again. President Trump blamed the nation of China, meaning the Chinese communist government, for the creation and spread of the global pandemic. The American left, to damage Trump politically, told the world that Trump is racist towards Chinese people. They redefined race to equate the original definition of the term with the Chinese Communist Party, as well as anyone that looks to be of Asian descent.

In doing this, the Democrats and the American left introduced the concept of racism to the narrative. It didn't exist until they invoked the notion and stoked the flames of racism. President Trump didn't do that. He never mentioned race at all. In fact, he clarified several times publicly that race had nothing to do with the Chinese Virus. The problem involved a series of actions by the leaders of the nation of China, our global adversary.

The American left introduced the concept of racism to the narrative, then accused President Trump of fomenting racism. From there, the willing accomplices in the media joined in on the false narrative and other dishonest leftist institutions (such as North Carolina State University) followed suit. That, my friends, is what redefining is all about. That's how it works. That's how the political left makes it work.

Imagine what America would have experienced if the Democrats and their collaborators on the political left had not invoked the dishonest racism narrative. Or imagine an honest media giving an accurate account of what President Trump told the world and shaming the American leftists for dishonest race-baiting politics. That could have happened, but it didn't then, and it wouldn't today, either.

Instead, we had duplicity from Democrat politicians,

media members, and academics. Instead, we were all subjected to the politics of race and racism from the usual suspects. Instead, we were bombarded with what seemed like endless choruses of "Trump's a racist" from the Democrats, the media, and perhaps their most insidious ally, academia.

Academia is supposed to be where predominantly young, impressionable Americans go to be educated and enlightened. Instead, we get to see what institutions such as North Carolina State University are "teaching" people. It's not an education if it stands counter to the relevant facts once known as truth.

Schools and universities that promote a political agenda that stands opposed to truth are neither educating nor enlightening anyone. They're indoctrinating students instead. And using false claims of racism adds a level of hatemongering to the mix. It's reprehensible. And they're too dishonest to even be ashamed of themselves.

WHITE-ADJACENT: As a subsection of this chapter, I'd like to discuss the somewhat recently "minted" phrase "White-adjacent." If you aren't sure what this phrase means, don't feel bad. As I researched this phrase, neither Merriam-Webster nor Dictionary.com, my typical "go-to" sites, showed an entry.

White-adjacent people are non-White people that are no longer considered as people of color. People of Asian descent are no longer being considered by many in society as typical minorities. They're too "White-ish." They're too "near-to White." Therefore, they're now White-adjacent.

Who came up with this nonsense and why? I'll bet you can guess. It was largely driven by academia and political think-tanks on the political left.

For quite some time now, the Asian demographic has been the "piss in the punch" for the race "hustlers." The American left has been selling everyone on the perpetual need to subsidize and/or legislate to relieve the burdensome plight of racial minorities in America.

For generations, we've been told that the livelihoods of people of color suffer disproportionately through no fault of their own because they lack the socioeconomic and educational opportunities of Whites. This has been the mantra for at least as long as I can remember. However, for quite some time, America has had at least one racial minority that has been consistently disproving the narrative.

Asian Americans are over-represented both educationally and socioeconomically in 21st Century America. By that, I mean statistically, they've over-achieved. This over-representation is especially high in the tech sector. As technology has developed, this demographic has flourished. Asian Americans now represent a relatively high-income demographic.

Asian Americans have been disproving the phony narrative on race in America for decades. Just as the race "pimps" are demonizing America as racist against people of color and selling lies of a society that keeps non-Whites down, we see Asians flourish. Why? It's simple. America isn't racist.

The primary factor keeping people down in America is their own behavior. Race isn't the determining factor for success in America. It's culture. It's learned behavior. Some behavior leads to success. Other behavior leads to failure. Behavior isn't the only factor. But it's the primary factor.

What does this have to do with redefining America? The overwhelming and growing success of Asian Americans in society has put leftist institutions and their friends that do their dirty work, the race hustlers, in a precarious position. As it has become harder to ignore the demographic that has so often and so obviously proven them wrong, they had to make a change. I'm sure some have since admitted to their intellectual folly. But most have chosen a more dishonest tactic. They've simply redefined what it means to be an Asian American.

The phrase White-adjacent was created so that leftists don't have to admit to being wrong about minorities in America. Seriously, imagine being a "respected institution of higher learning" and having to admit that your demographic studies over the years are inherently flawed. No. They had a better idea. Rather than continuing to consider Asians as non-White or people of color and a racial minority, they decided to simply categorize them along with Whites as White-adjacent.

Just like that, POOF! Asian Americans, you *were* non-White. You *used to be* a racial minority. Not anymore. Now you're "White-ish." You're "White enough." You're White-adjacent. You're no longer a minority in America. You've become part of the racial majority as a matter of convenience for the political left.

We simply *must* have this new category of White-adjacent so that leftist institutions and think-tanks don't have to admit that their studies were and are wrong. Nor do left-wing Democrat politicians have to admit to being wrong. Nor do Al Sharpton, Jesse Jackson, and the rest of the race-baiting left. It works as a necessity for the entire leftist cabal.

What's the purpose of redefining race and racism? It's being done for much the same reason and purpose that we saw with the concept of truth. It's being done to demonize and ultimately shut down those that stand in opposition.

Actual racism is hate-driven bigotry that isn't nor should be tolerated. Americans overwhelmingly agree on this principle. That's why I argue that America is not a racist nation. We spend little time, if any, defending what's universally understood to be racist. So, then, why do we still have an undeniable racial division in America?

We have racial division because of the *politics* of race. We have division because we have one political ideology using race as a wedge to gain political support. We have a leftist ideology that has weaponized the issue to bludgeon their political adversaries. And we have it because it works. It's easy and effective.

You know how this goes. We've all been witness to it for decades. If you disagree with a member of the Democrat party, the party of leftism, on anything involving race, you're a racist. Even if you disagree with a leftist Democrat on something that doesn't involve race, you're still a racist if they say so. It's so convoluted now that even Black conservatives are labelled as racist if a prominent Democrat says so.

Here's an example. In an Axios piece from October 2022, titled "J.D. Vance and Tim Ryan Spar Over Racism in Senate Debate." Democrat candidate Ryan accused Republican candidate Vance of supporting closing our southern border because according to Ryan, Vance believes in the "White replacement theory." This means Vance is allegedly afraid that too many people of color (such as his wife and children, ironically) are going to replace White people (such as himself) and circumvent their control over our nation. It's no wonder Ryan lost the election to Vance. Ohioans didn't buy into the lie.

Like I said, this is easy. American leftists from one institution to another say that if you don't believe in an open border, it's because you don't want brown-skinned people in the country "replacing" White people. In other words, it's because you're racist. Following the law and securing the border is racist, according to dishonest Democrats that can benefit by weaponizing the issue of race.

And on and on it goes. Don't be a racist. Be a Democrat. Right? Can you sense the sarcasm?

3

Illegal/Undocumented

D on't call them "illegals." "No human being is illegal," according to the political left. The focus of this chapter is regarding illegal immigration and the redefining of such a concept.

According to one, Isabel Johnston, in a piece titled: "Words Matter: No Human Being is Illegal" from the blog *Immigration and Human Rights Law Review*, we get another highbrow "intellectual" viewpoint on the subject:

> A person cannot be illegal. While certain actions may be criminal, or illegal, people cannot be illegal. Although in the US, it is a federal crime to enter the country without inspection, it is not a crime to be present within the country without authorization. Thus, a person living in the US without status, or without a valid visa, is not committing a crime.

Isn't that interesting? Luckily for us, we can always find "intellectuals" to assist us as we try to advance ourselves to likewise achieve their "higher level of understanding." Let's give this a deeper look.

According to Dictionary.com, the term "illegal" is an adjective meaning, *"forbidden by law or statute."* This is a wonderfully simple, straightforward definition and undoubtably the most common understanding of the term.

People cannot be illegal or illegals. This is true. The term is generally understood to be an adjective, not a noun. Therefore, technically, she's right. An adjective is a word that describes or modifies a noun. It's descriptive. It isn't a thing. It describes a thing.

Let me clarify this another way. This is a distinction without a difference. As the author states, a person living in the United States without proper status isn't *commiting* a crime. Rather, they had already *committed* a crime upon illegal entry. Get it?

I suppose technically, she's right in her statement. But it misses the substance of the term entirely, by design. Referring to someone as an illegal is grammatically incorrect but substantively accurate. She and the rest of the dishonest leftist cabal are deceitful in using grammar and past versus present tense to redefine this concept. We understand the phrase "illegal alien" to mean someone, a noncitizen, that entered the country illegally.

We understand the phrase illegal alien perfectly well, conceptually. I presume the phrase was shortened to "illegals" to incorporate brevity and to avoid the term "alien." I can clearly recall a time not too long ago in which the left was "campaigning" for the purging of the term alien from our lexicon. It was too "mean spirited" a word, we were told. Now, we aren't supposed to call them aliens or illegal despite the fact that they represent the very definition of *illegal aliens.*

Remember, the political left is playing a semantical game with us not for the purpose of clearly defining and qualifying relevant terms for a more advanced level of understanding, but for the opposite effect. This is another such example.

People that came to America illegally are criminals. They broke the law upon entry at the very least. This is a fact despite the "word salad" and the attempted sanitization of the term illegal by the political left.

Why are they redefining the term illegal or illegals (as well as aliens)? It's because they want open borders and an influx of immigrants regardless of legality. They don't like our border laws and want people to be sympathetic to any migration, legal or illegal. They want us to believe as they do, that there should be no such thing as illegal immigration and that America should be open to anyone and everyone that wants to be a citizen. It's another leftist sales job as they sell their contrived narrative.

"They aren't really illegal." "It isn't a crime for them to be present in the country." "Living in the country without status is not committing a crime." These utterances are revealing in that they show how leftists are working to manipulate American law. These quotes all represent intentional deception. Intentional deception is the precise definition of a *lie*.

What does the term "undocumented" mean? According to Dictionary.com, it means: "1. Lacking documentation or authentication. 2. Lacking proper immigration or working papers." What's the difference between someone being considered as illegal versus being undocumented?

A person that entered America illegally is a criminal according to federal law. They committed a criminal act regardless of whether or not the leftist politician, media pundit, judge or justice, or academic wants to admit it. But being undocumented...that's different. Being undocumented can be easily and conveniently explained away by the aforementioned leftists.

The political left wants us to believe that undocumented people aren't criminals. They're just meager folks from different cultures that speak different languages having understandable difficulties managing our somewhat complex immigration system. They just need help "dotting the i's and crossing the t's" as we get them proper documentation. While criminals may belong in jail, undocumented people just need our help.

The "open borders crowd" on the political left is redefining what it means to be illegal (or an alien) in America. Just as we've seen with other terms and phrases, they refuse to acknowledge facts and truth that stand opposed to their radical ideology. To the political left, the end justifies the means. The lies and duplicity aren't what matters to them. It's about affecting change upon America whether we want it or not. It's about moving America more towards a leftist utopian world view.

4

Asylum Seekers

We have a mess at our southern border. It's truly a crisis and it's out of control. There are numerous reasons for which we cannot control our southern border. One such reason is because many of our leaders are simply lying to everyone about who's showing up at our doorsteps and for what purpose. We have a group of duly elected leaders that have redefined what they're calling "asylum seekers" precisely to confuse and trick the American public into believing a dishonest political narrative.

Do the masses of humanity that are rushing to (primarily) our southern border qualify as asylum seekers or are they migrants? We'll get to that distinction as the chapter unfolds. And is there an appreciable difference between the two classifications?

The answer to that question is a resounding YES! There's a tremendous difference both morally and legally between asylum seekers and (economic) migrants.

Let's define our terms. According to Dictionary.com, an asylum seeker is defined as, "a person, especially a political fugitive, who applies for refuge or asylum in a foreign country or its embassy." I feel as if I should apologize for going to Wikipedia for a definition (to be taken seriously), but they actually did a fantastic job to further qualify the concept.

Once again, I will refer to *The Freedom Prescription* to help define and differentiate the concepts of asylum seekers versus migrants:

> What's an asylum seeker? And, what's a migrant? According to Wikipedia, 'An asylum seeker is a person who flees their home country, enters another country and applies for asylum, i.e. the right to international protection, in this other country. An asylum seeker is a type of migrant and may be a refugee, a displaced person, but not an economic migrant.' Here's the gist of the matter: Asylum seekers are fleeing persecution from government forces in their homeland. Again, that's GOVERNMENT FORCES. Not family members. Not local criminals or gangs.
>
> Asylum seekers claim refugee status upon arrival at our border. What's a refugee? According to The United Nations, 'Refugees are people who cannot return to their country of origin because of a well-founded fear of persecution, conflict, violence, or other circumstances that have seriously disturbed public order, and who, as a result, require international protection.

Now, here's the rub. Almost none of the so-called asylum-seeking migrants coming to our border(s) meet these U.N. designated qualifications. In other words, they're showing up and falsely claiming refugee status as asylum seekers. They're being coached "en masse" to lie about their status. They're being taught to file false claims so that they can use both our own laws and international laws to fight being shipped back home.

Almost all of them are economic migrants. They came for work. The majority of them are lying and cheating the system to try to get in without going through the proper process. Most Americans, such as I, have no problem with taking in migrant workers the right way, under our terms. Instead, we're being "bum rushed," overwhelmed, and lied to. They're taking advantage of our laws, our charity, and our humanity. What they're doing is wrong and it's greatly harming America. Unsurprisingly, our friends on the political left are their enablers.

Understand that when we hear someone from the political left refer to the hordes of migrants "rushing" our border as asylum seekers, they're either ignorant or they're lying to us. I'm sure some are ignorant. However, most of them know exactly what they're doing. They're knowingly promoting a falsely contrived narrative. They're lying to us.

Do you need some examples? There are countless stories about asylum seekers all over the internet and traditional "news" outlets. I readily (and randomly) pulled one up from Buzzfeed News. They chronicle what's happening at our southern border in what they call *Beyond Migrant*.

According to buzzfeednews.com,

> *Beyond Migrant* is a series of portraits of families who have gotten caught in the limbo of US immigration policies and been sent to Mexico after trying to seek asylum.

I'd like to focus on a few of their chosen examples of so-called asylum seekers to show how they're being portrayed to the world. Remember, these particular examples are folks that had been caught illegally entering the U.S. and were sent to Mexico after petitioning for asylum in America.

From Buzzfeed's Pia Peterson and Hailey Sadler, in an article titled "You Want To See Your Child 'Grow Up': Asylum-Seekers Sent Back To Mexico Share Their Stories," posted on July 28, 2021:

> Oscar Pineda,...and his son...have been living in limbo in Mexicali for a little over three years. A mechanic by

trade, Pineda fled his home country of Honduras after being targeted by a local gang.

According to the article, Mr. Pineda openly stated that he was fleeing from a gang. That does not qualify him for asylum from Honduras. Therefore, he is not an asylum seeker. Period.

Next, we had the story of another Honduran; a woman named Vilma Peraza. According to the article,

> As a single mom, she made the difficult decision to leave her home with a migrant caravan in 2018, in hopes of being able to fight for a better future for her children in the United States.

Her somewhat lengthy story made no mention of any sort of persecution in her homeland. It seems she wants nothing more than a better life, so she claimed asylum. But where's the allegation of any type of persecution? Buzzfeed never poses that obvious and crucial question as they go from one story to the next.

As a matter of fact, that seems to be the case over and over again. In countless articles from so-called news sources, opinion pieces or from the talking heads in the political arena, it seems precious few advocates for whom they like to call asylum seekers ever mention the existence of governmental persecution from which they flee. How can that be?

Am I the only person that sits in front of their television or smart device asking the video image of a talking head (admittedly, very much like a mental patient) that has no way to comprehend my retorts, "Well...you just said that these asylum seekers are primarily coming from Central America. So, tell us, which governments of what Central American countries are persecuting their citizens?!"

Isn't that the question every viewer or reader should be asking every time they absorb one of these stories and political narratives? For that matter, shouldn't the "journalists" that author these stories answer to this hypocrisy. No. Because they aren't actual journalists. Instead, they work as "sales representatives" for the political left.

If these migrants are asylum seekers, which governments of what countries are guilty of persecuting their own citizens and precisely how so? Can't someone ask these absolutely fundamental questions?

Again, am I the only one that has been asking (for years) how we can have literally millions of people from many dozens of countries showing up at our border claiming that they have a "well-founded fear of persecution, conflict, violence, or other circumstances that have seriously disturbed public order, and who, as a result, require international protection?" Most of the illegal immigrants come from Central American nations. Yet, outside of Cuba and more recently Haiti, what Pan-American countries have been engaging in that kind of mistreatment of their citizenry?

In other words, do any of these people, these examples, these cases, actually represent individuals seeking asylum? In almost every instance the answer is no.

This simply doesn't add up. We're persistently being told that there are millions of abused people that need to be protected by America. Who, then, are the abusers? Have you heard testimony from so-called asylum seekers that the governments of Honduras or Mexico or El Salvador or Nicaragua are persecuting their citizens to the point of driving them out of their homelands by the tens of thousands at a time?

Those are the inherent and necessary allegations when anyone claims asylum. They're laying sworn testimonials to such circumstances for legal adjudication. They're testifying that this is the reality within their homeland(s) that drove them to our border. Yet, where's that type of evidence?

Not only does Buzzfeed and so many other purveyors of the false asylum narrative not give any such evidence, but they also ignore the fact that such evidence is a necessary component at all. Here's the key point my friends: They've redefined the term asylum to no longer mean its once universally understood definition.

The fact of the matter is that nearly all these so-called asylum seekers, these so-called refugees, are nothing of the sort. Yet, leftists from the media and the political class insist on routinely referring to them as such. Why? As is typical, the truth is antithetical to their dishonest narrative. The truth of the matter is that nearly all of these "pilgrims" are here for another reason.

What does it infer to everyone when millions of people are willing to travel hundreds or thousands of miles enduring so much of the dangers, costs, and hardships along the way as many of them pass through one "safe" nation after the next? What does it tell you that so many of them verbally state outright for the record that they're coming to America for a better life just before and even sometimes after claiming asylum protection under U. S. and international law? It tells us that the asylum and refugee claims are almost all a big lie. That's what it should demonstrate to any clear-thinking human being.

Now, why is it so important for the political left to redefine what it means to be an asylum seeker and/or refugee? To adhere to the beliefs of the political left in America, we all must share their conclusion that anyone on the face of the earth that wants to be an American has the moral and legal right to lie about their status and claim the right to some form of American citizenship or right thereof, upon arrival.

It's the redefining of the terms asylum and refugee by the political left to include economic migrants that grants the absolute (legal) right to show up at our border and lie to us about being persecuted by their government. And, according to the political left, there's nothing we can do both legally and morally but to let them stay.

That's the end game. That's much of the "who, how, and why" many factions in America have been working to redefine these terms and concepts. That's a big part of understanding the intentional state of chaos at (primarily) our southern border. And our disastrous border and immigration policies are what we get when the political left wins the day.

5

Infrastructure

A s I wrote this chapter, the Democrats controlled the White House along with both chambers of Congress. There was heated debate among politicians, partisans, and pundits regarding infrastructure legislation. Significant infrastructure spending was imminent.

But precisely what qualifies as "infrastructure"? The term infrastructure is defined by Merriam-Webster as: "1: the system of public works of a country, state, or region. 2: the underlying foundation or basic framework. 3: the permanent installations required for military purposes."

They go on to further describe the term as follows:

> Infra-means "below"; so the infrastructure is the "underlying structure" of a country and its economy, the fixed installations that it needs in order to function. These include roads, bridges, dams, the water and sewer systems, railways and subways, airports, and harbors. These are generally government-built and publicly owned.

The Merriam-Webster definition, explanation, and examples represent the commonly understood concept of infrastructure. However, does that represent the same concept of infrastructure that's typically being debated by our political class and punditry, then sold to America?

Throughout much of 2021, Congress, along with President Biden, was crafting, debating and working toward the eventual passage of a massive infrastructure bill. Let's look at some of what the political left was selling as infrastructure in what they were calling their infrastructure bill.

Fox Business published an article titled "Infrastructure bill's unusual provisions: Drunk driving tech mandate to 'pollinator-friendly' roads," in which they detail some of the other provisions in the bill. The bill included an "equity assessment" that would, "give grants to nonprofits and state and local governments for the purpose of making urban areas more environmentally friendly."

It included drunk driving detection equipment for automobiles that can shut off the vehicle if the driver has alcohol on their breath. It included the creation of a "Women of Trucking Advisory Board." It would also give out grants to plant wildflowers on roadsides, remove "nonnative grasses," and to pay consulting fees for advice on pollinator-friendly roadside management.

These are some of the so-called infrastructure measures within what was at the time a multi-trillion dollar, 2700-page bill. That's a debt and deficit ballooning 2700 pages of pork and crap that nobody can possibly predict or understand in totality its ramifications.

I know what you're thinking. Shoving additional spending initiatives into bills doesn't amount to the redefining of a basic term or concept. Adding "pork" to bills and "bringing home the bacon" from D. C. is business as usual in Washington and practiced by both sides of the political aisle. Hang on. There's more to it than that. As you'll see in the next few articles, this went beyond business as usual in our nation's capital.

Here's an excerpt from a piece from the *New York Post*

written by Tamar Lapin on April 7, 2021, titled "'Unicorns are infrastructure': Sen. Gillibrand mocked for definition of Biden plan":

> in a push for President Biden's massive $2.3 trillion tax-and-spend plan, the New York Democrat attempted to pave a new meaning, tweeting: 'Paid leave is infrastructure. Childcare is infrastructure. Caregiving is infrastructure.'

In an article written by David Keltz from the *American Spectator*, on April 12, 2021, titled "Everything Is Infrastructure, Democrats redefine the word to promote an American Jobs Plan that is anything but," the writer pretty much nails my point:

> On Friday, Transportation Secretary Pete Buttigieg held his first press briefing at the White House to pitch President Biden's $2.3 trillion infrastructure plan. Buttigieg, ever the salesman, described the so-called American Jobs Plan (AJP) as "the best chance in our lifetimes to make a generational investment in infrastructure." In order to sell this non-infrastructure bill, Buttigieg has had to redefine the word 'infrastructure.' On Sunday, Buttigieg was asked by CNN's Jake Tapper if Republicans could undermine the legislation by calling it a pork barrel of left-wing social programs disguised as an infrastructure bill. Buttigieg responded with this:
> "I very much believe that all of these things are infrastructure, because infrastructure is the foundation that allows us to go about our lives…. To me, it makes no sense to say, I would have been for broadband, but I'm against it because it's not a bridge. I would have been for eldercare, but I'm against it because it's not a highway."

That's a sophist's way of saying that infrastructure

means whatever he and the Biden administration want it to mean. Buttigieg disingenuously claims that those who do not support federal funding for eldercare in an 'infrastructure' bill are somehow against helping senior citizens, when in reality they oppose being sold a bill that isn't as advertised.

In a piece from the *Independent*, by Gustav Kilander, on August 17, 2021, titled: "'We have a moral obligation': Democrats consider using infrastructure money for Afghan refugees," Mr. Kilander wrote:

> Some congressional Democrats are exploring the option of using some of the money from their proposed $3.5 trillion infrastructure reconciliation bill for the resettlement of Afghan refugees.

That's their idea of infrastructure.

Do you see the difference? This is more than a $3.5 trillion all-you-can-eat pork buffet. This is another example of the redefining of a basic term to win a political narrative and garner popular support for legislation that will ultimately affect all Americans. This involved a coordinated political strategy to change the conceptual meaning of the term infrastructure to include within its definition a virtual cornucopia of left-wing approved agenda items and pet projects.

This dishonest political strategy attempts to equate taxpayer-funded charity for Afghan refugees to securing Americas roads and bridges as if they're somehow comparable. This dishonest strategy attempts to equate the American left's choice for eldercare to the maintenance of airports, seaports, subways, and rail service. These dishonest politicians and their mouthpieces are selling the narrative that childcare and the government funding of a "Women of Trucking Advisory Board" somehow equates to the maintenance of water and sewer systems. Why?

Because, according to those redefining infrastructure, if you're against their pork-laden, budget busting, big-government empowering, liberty choking, left-wing agenda, then you must also be against maintaining traditional infrastructure such as roads, bridges, airports, seaports, etc. Again, according to the left, if you stand opposed to the full litany of the left-wing social spending projects packed within the 2700 plus pages of the bill at a cost estimated around $3.5 trillion, you're against fixing America's infrastructure.

Are you buying into this?

Anyone that concedes to the newly fabricated definition of infrastructure, must equate the American left's political agenda to traditional infrastructure. And, by equate, I mean that we can't have one without the other. If infrastructure now includes whatever the liberal Democrats in power want it to mean, then no Americans can be against their political agenda without also being against securing roads, bridges, ports, etc.

They redefined the term infrastructure to conflate two different sets of agenda items. One is a set of important and necessary measures that America cannot function without, and the other is a set of agenda items that reflect a socialistic utopia that will further grow and empower the federal government while also crushing our economy

That was the plan. That was the coordinated political strategy behind the redefining of the term and concept of infrastructure by the political left in America.

6
Entitlements

U nlike many of the other redefined terms we'll cover in this book, the term "entitlement" is one that was successfully redefined by our political class long ago. What's an entitlement? Once again, I'm going to refer to my earlier composition, *The Freedom Prescription*, for our working definition and some relevant thoughts:

> What's an entitlement? Merriam-Webster has a few definitions. The first, and I'll wager the original definition, is a noun meaning: "the condition of having a right to have, do, or get something." Under this definition, an entitlement is a right. Merriam-Webster followed that definition with two others: "The feeling or belief that you deserve to be given something (such as special privileges)," and "A type of financial help provided by the government for members of a particular group." Putting all of this together, you get a group of citizens with special privileges that have the right (real or perceived) to taxpayer funded subsidies.

I like how Merriam-Webster defines this term because they

come right out with what I call the universally understood definition first; as they should. Then, unfortunately, they get all "squishy." Don't misunderstand my sentiment. It's not meant as a critique. They did an admirable job including and qualifying the "new" definition(s) that has become so popular to the political left in America. However, this leaves us with a few very different definitions and/or qualifications. And the differences are stark.

The first definition, the one that I consider the universally understood definition, requires that someone has the "right" to have or to get something—meaning that to be deemed as entitled to something, one must have a right to it. This requires a *justification.*

For example, Americans have the right to a federal tax return for overpayment of federal taxes. This is what I like to call a "true" entitlement. A federal tax return for overpayment is a justifiable right. That's because it's every American's right to the return of their own money if they paid more than they were required to pay. It's their own (earned) money. This example clearly demonstrates what should be considered as a true entitlement.

Now, let's take a look at what happens when we incorporate what I call the new part of the definition. Under the newer definition, one becomes entitled to something by simply feeling or believing that they deserve something. Under this definition, no longer does there need to be any kind of right or justification to an entitlement beyond just feelings and beliefs. And the so-called entitlement is granted in the form of financial assistance from the government directed to a particular group.

We're going to need to break this down further. Think about it. There are true entitlements that fit the first of Webster's definitions that don't broach upon the others. This is fundamental; a true entitlement is one that affords a right to someone, but that doesn't require either property or service from someone else nor a right to be taken from someone else. You aren't truly entitled to something if it comes at a cost to someone else. Again, that's fundamental.

How does one become entitled? The answer to that question holds the key to the point of this chapter. We have literally millions of people at any given time that are receiving so-called entitlement subsidies from different levels of government. What must folks do to receive an entitlement subsidy? And, from whom and/or where do the funds for all these entitlements derive?

There's all the difference in the world between Webster's first definition, a true entitlement, and what we now hear our government sector and so many others refer to as entitlements. The new definition of entitlement does something very interesting with the concept of having the right to an entitlement. You see, with the first definition and corresponding example (tax return), there was a right to the entitlement because the money from the entitlement originally came from the recipient. It was a return of *their own money.*

Under the new definition, how does one become entitled? The answer is two-fold. In most cases it solely comes down to *need*. People simply "need it." For example, if you can't afford a home but need one, you're entitled to government subsidized housing. If you can't afford food but need to eat and perhaps feed your dependents, you're entitled to government subsidized food. The same can apply for educational needs, healthcare, and on and on. One becomes entitled by simply being in a state of need.

In other cases, some people just feel or believe that they or others deserve entitlements because they believe that those with an abundance don't deserve their fortunate circumstance. After all, it's a matter of "fairness." For example, "White privilege" is inherently unfair, we're told by leftists. Therefore, they believe that people of color deserve to be compensated by White folks (see, reparations and affirmative action).

Government-imposed wealth redistribution, a bastion of American leftist policy and orthodoxy, in all its forms, is predicated on the fundamental assertion that those with "too much" don't *deserve* to keep it. And, conversely, those in *need* should have it redistributed to them to provide care for their needs.

From all of this comes the redefining of the concept of entitlement(s). The new definition is built on the moral high ground of (so-called) fairness and taking care of the needs of others. This is a narrative that many find difficult to oppose for obvious reasons. Who would want to stand in opposition to fairness and taking care of the needy? It's easy to see why the American left was so successful at redefining the term, entitlement.

As is typically the case with leftist policies, they sound good. They make lots of folks feel good about themselves and the society that they reformed. Sadly, they also create disastrous results that the architects refuse to acknowledge.

The "entitlement society" of 21st Century America involves a national debt of nearly $40 trillion as more Americans learn that it pays "well enough" to be needy. Why work hard? Why sacrifice? Where's the need to be productive? And why take risks as an entrepreneur? The more successful you become, the more you'll have confiscated from you for the common good of the so-called needy.

Does a society become moral or equitable by claiming the right to the fruits of the labor of someone else? Are you entitled to the goods and/or services, the work, of someone else? For example, do you have the right to free healthcare? Let me rephrase that question. Do you have the right to force your healthcare providers to administer service to you for free? How do you force someone to work for you without compensating them? Seriously, how is that done, at gunpoint?

For decades, leftist Democrats have been telling millions of Americans that they're owed something and that someone else is going to pay for it. Is this sound policy? Or is it pandering at its worst?

Democrats and the American left force their so-called

entitlement policies upon America through uncontrolled debt (and deficits) and through wealth confiscation in the name of fairness and equity. But is it really fair and equitable to bury future generations under the burdensome debt of their predecessors?

Furthermore, is it moral, equitable or even legal to help yourself to the funds within your neighbor's bank account? It certainly isn't. Finally, if it's unjust for you to unilaterally take what belongs to your neighbor (against their will), then why would you believe that it's fair or just to send the government to do the same?

Think about those questions because that's precisely what's happening with what's being defined as entitlements in America today.

7
Liberal/Liberalism

What does it mean to be a "liberal"? Notice, I'm referring to a liberal as in a noun, not an adjective. For a person to fit the definition of a liberal, what characteristics must they possess? According to Merriam-Webster, the definition of liberal as a noun, is:

> one who is open-minded or not strict in the observance of orthodox, traditional, or established forms or ways, (b) a member or supporter of a liberal political party, (c) an advocate or adherent of liberalism especially in individual rights.

So, a liberal, by definition, is someone that is not tied to a particular orthodoxy, tradition, or establishment and that advocates for individual rights or liberty. Isn't that interesting? That doesn't seem to fit the description of many liberals I know.

As most everyone knows, the American left refers to themselves as liberals. And, naturally, they expect the rest of us to describe them as such. This, in my mind, poses two immediate questions. Is that an accurate description of the American left? And why do they choose or wish to be described in that way?

Let's consider and parse the second question first. Why would the American left or anyone, for that matter, wish to be considered as a liberal? It's because a liberal is defined as a person with an open-minded philosophy that is accepting of the differences of others regardless of their own personal belief constructs. That's because a liberal person, by definition, believes in granting to others the right to believe as they so choose.

This means that liberals are open to accepting differing points of view. Liberals promote liberty. Isn't that a good thing? I would contend that adhering to the philosophical traits described and defined by Merriam-Webster as liberal are positive, indeed. Sign me up, please! I love these concepts! I must be a liberal, right?

Now, back to the first question. Are America's leftists, the so-called and self-proclaimed American liberals, *really* liberal? Let's delve into that question by examining issues of the day. We can go issue by issue and ultimately determine where the American left stands regarding prescribed policies and direction for America. We'll use some of the most hotly debated issues of our time.

Regarding taxes, the American left supports high (confiscatory) taxes and deficit spending. Turning over a large percentage of one's earnings to government forces (most often against one's will) does not promote liberty. And being saddled with the debt of others, including one's predecessors, is truly the antithesis of liberty. It's really a form of economic slavery.

In fairness, historically speaking, Republicans have also been terrible at fiscal constraint. The Republican party is also responsible for our debt crisis. However, the conservative faction of the party is not. Conservative Republicans are traditionally and historically the ones fighting for fiscal responsibility typically in a losing effort. Conservatives simply cannot be expected to defeat the entire Democrat contingency along with the big government and globalist Republicans within their own ranks.

The American left's social policies of affirmative action and racial politics based on perceived entitlements divides Americans into racial groups with the intention of taking from one group to redistribute to another to "make up for" historical indiscretions.

This is a prime example of the American left forcing their radical orthodoxy upon all Americans. Perhaps even more egregious is the notion that anyone living today should be punished for the "sins" of others from America's past.

A forced political orthodoxy and forced monetary redistribution (from those that freely earned it) is grossly antithetical to the basic concept of liberalism.

The American left has been pushing towards forcing all Americans into a socialized medicine program which would fundamentally change the relationship between the citizen and government. Instead of healthcare choices being between an individual and their doctor with the government as arbitrator, the government would decide who gets what care and when. If you don't believe me, look at COVID-19 vaccine mandates and Democrats proposing to withhold healthcare from those that don't comply. You'll do what you're told or else, say the...*liberals*?

Cancel culture and political correctness also come from the American left. As Dictionary.com defines it:

> Cancel culture refers to the popular practice of withdrawing support for public figures and companies after they have done or said something considered objectionable or offensive.

They also describe it as "group shaming."

Political correctness or being "woke" is the American left's thought police. The American left has taken to shaming individuals and groups that don't adhere to their leftist political orthodoxy with the stated goal of destroying businesses and careers as well as humiliating those that dissent. I ask you, does that behavior in any way fit the definition of liberal?

One simply cannot discuss the policies and vision of the American left without mentioning socialism. Somewhat recently, socialism has become mainstream for the political left. For anyone that doesn't understand this concept, in its basic form, socialism is collectivism. At its core, socialism is about empowering the masses collectively through the repudiation of individualism. The needs of the many outweigh the rights of the individual.

That's the premise and philosophical justification of the concept of socialism. How does that fit with the definition of liberalism and more specifically, Merriam-Webster's, "(c) an advocate or adherent of liberalism especially in individual rights?" According to our socialist friends on the left, individuals shouldn't have rights that supersede collective needs. Once again, the policies and philosophies of the American left directly oppose the essential meaning of liberty and liberalism.

The concept of liberalism was hijacked, twisted, and redefined by the American left decades ago. Although this is old news conceptually speaking, over time we experience more examples and instances of the left's debasement of the term. There are new examples daily of representatives from the American left turning their backs on the concepts of open-mindedness, inclusivity, tolerance, and individual liberty.

The political left in America like to describe themselves as liberals. As you can see, their redefining of the term twists its meaning into a complete falsehood.

8

Hate

How has the concept or definition of "hate" changed over recent time? Follow me here. It's not so much the actual and universally understood definition of hate that has changed. It's what *constitutes or qualifies* as hate that has changed. And it's the politics of hate and the weaponization of this concept that has led America down a destructive path.

Let's define hate. According to Dictionary.com, hate means: "to dislike intensely or passionately; feel extreme aversion for or extreme hostility toward; detest." As I alluded to earlier, the working definition of the term isn't the crux of the issue. I'm fine with it. The problematic change is in its application.

The change resides in determining what actions, words or even thoughts are now deemed to qualify as hate or hateful. Conceptually, hate has always been an arbitrary construct. What's deemed as hateful by one person may not be considered to be hateful by another. Furthermore, an action that might have initially been considered as hateful may have an explanation or unknown circumstance that would make the same person that had initially deemed it as hateful to change their mind and understand it as otherwise.

For these reasons, even with a static and universally accepted definition, this concept is fluid, as it's applied over time, incident, and circumstances. It's within this arbitrary qualification and application that the so-called redefining of hate is being done.

If we really want to understand the redefined meaning of hate, we need to delve into the politics of hate. Sadly, in 21st Century America, we can't turn on the television, radio, or join social media without being constantly bombarded with the politics of hate from all over the spectrum, especially by our media curators.

There's a political strategy being implemented by the American left using hate as a tool. It's simple, and it works like this: any and every issue of the day has two sides or factions. You have the side of righteousness, and you have the side of hate. Their prevailing narrative will always find the American left and Democrat leaders on the side of righteousness and conservative leaders, most especially President Trump, on the side of hate.

As a matter of strategy, conservatives and President Trump are always portrayed as the purveyors of hate. According to the American left, every policy decision by conservatives is driven by their hate for someone or something. *Always*. Gone is the notion that there can be two sides to any debate or disagreement outside of the relatively new binary certitudes of righteousness and/or hate. It's good versus evil. It's as if there's absolutely no legitimate reason to oppose the far left's radical agenda(s) other than hate.

Let's recall a few examples of such behavior from recent discussions and debates over current issues from the not-so-distant past. According to leading leftists in the media, the leftist political class, and the Hollywood left, President Trump and conservatives want a secure southern border with a physical border wall because they hate "brown" people.

That's what the left still routinely tries to pass as thoughtful mainstream political commentary regarding the mess that is our southern border.

Allegedly, President Trump and his conservative supporters are against affirmative action and support our law enforcement officers because they're racist (hateful) towards African Americans.

Also, Trump and his conservative supporters favor cutting taxes because they hate poor people and want to help their rich friends.

Again, these are just a few examples of what passes as thoughtful political commentary from the "experts" on the left. Forget about examining both sides of an issue or the merits of the debate. No such things exist, according to many on the political left. After their dishonest portrayal of what typically constitutes the majority of Americans that disagree with their radical agenda, those in opposition to the American left are labeled as hateful and divisive. This is the politics of hate in America today. This is how hate is qualified and thus, newly defined.

As I detailed in *The Freedom Prescription*, be on guard as minions from the political left have been trying to use the legislative process and existing law to actually criminalize their new definition of hate. This is the essence of Hate Crimes Legislature.

Just imagine if the American left could legislate against what they consider as hate. Would you publicly stand opposed to such a notion? Aren't you against hate? Shouldn't we all stand proudly alongside Democrat leaders as they do their level best to rid America of hate? "Just which side are you on, pal? Are you for righteousness or do you stand for hate?" Won't that be the narrative we can expect if this movement grows to reach the forefront of American politics?

Just think about what would happen if the American left could criminalize hate. What would happen to our nation if they were able to arbitrarily qualify, criminalize and ultimately punish hate?

How would Nancy Pelosi or CNN or the *New York Times* define and qualify hate? Aren't they on record telling us that wearing a "Make America Great Again" hat is hateful? According to many Democrats, isn't simply being a Republican hateful? I've heard that stated countless times from the leftist talking heads in the media and from sitting Democrats in Congress. Can these things be criminalized? Why not?

I have an idea—let's just stay far away from this leftist notion of legislating hate. It has the makings of a Pandora's Box. While we're at it, let's all recognize the ongoing attempt by the American left to "corner the market" on righteousness by reconstituting the concept of hate and conveniently laying such an indictment on their adversaries. It's just another phony leftist narrative. Hate should not be defined or qualified as "those against the political wishes of the radical left in America."

While we're at it, let's also acknowledge the damage that this political narrative is doing to our nation. Sadly, hate is an effective tool and/or political weapon. It works. In 2020, it helped the Democrats defeat President Trump's re-election bid. He was defeated on the politics of personal destruction rather than his policies. Those that stood against his re-election typically did so with a searing hatred towards him personally.

If you don't believe me, just ask. Find a Trump hater. It won't take much effort. I promise. Ask them why they hate President Trump. Then see how long it takes for them to mention even one *policy-related* point of dissension. They will almost certainly spew back any and all of the allegations they can recall from one left-wing media driven personal attack to the next.

They have an irrational personal hatred for a leader that moved America forward in ways too numerous to take the time to list. Instead, they're blinded by their hatred for things that he did or said that were sometimes wrong along with baseless allegations (both impeachments as examples) that they simply want and choose to believe.

A sizable number of Americans have been virtually spoon-fed the unrelenting hate that comes from our left-wing dominated media to the point that they don't even consider the issues and policies of the Trump Administration as important regarding his re-election and governance. They just hate him. "Orange man bad!"

Again, just get the "Never Trumpers" barking and listen for yourself. Determine for yourself, do they seem to present a logical case for why the opposing candidate was a better choice for America? Or, rather, do they display the characteristics of people that have swallowed and consumed the irrational politics of hate "hook, line, and sinker?" Do they try to win you over with a better vision? Or do they attempt to emotionally rationalize *their own* irrational hate? You decide.

The politics of hate works, but at what cost? It's a scorched-earth approach. It leaves Americans angry, resentful, and divided. Although it should be a "bridge too far," it's more like politics as usual. It's important that Americans recognize the tactic, and which party is making use of it. And it helps to understand why it's being perpetrated on Americans.

The great irony here is that the left uses allegations of hatred and divisiveness by their political opponent(s) to incite hatred and divisiveness from their supporters. Think about that. Then, they direct the hatred and divisiveness t*hat they've sown* towards their adversaries while blaming their adversaries for fomenting all the hatred and divisiveness.

Did that last paragraph give you vertigo? Read it again. Get it now? I hope so.

9
Nationalism

When did the term "nationalism" become a dirty word? Hold that thought. We'll get back to that. According to Dictionary.com, nationalism is a noun and has several possible definitions:

1 Spirit or aspirations common to the whole of a nation. 2 Devotion and loyalty to one's own country; patriotism. 3 Excessive patriotism; chauvinism. 4 The desire for national advancement or political independence. 5 The policy or doctrine of asserting the interest of one's own nation viewed as separate from the interest of other nations or the common interest of all nations. 6 An idiom or trait peculiar to a nation. 7 A movement, as in the arts, based upon the folk idioms, history, aspirations, etc., of a nation.

That's certainly a large and cumbersome definition. I know, there's a lot to "unpack" here. I like how Dictionary. com defines this term because it's a very comprehensive definition. This helps us to better understand when folks are using it accurately versus those twisting its universally understood meaning perhaps for nefarious purposes.

How were you "brought up" or formally educated to understand the meaning of nationalism? I remember how it was taught to me as a student in my formative years. I was taught that nationalism was synonymous with patriotism. This would equate to Dictionary.com's definition number two. I expect that most other Americans from my generation and older share a similar understanding of this term.

Let's go back to Dictionary.com's seven related concepts that combine to define nationalism. The first two parts of the definition best match what my classmates and I were taught in school. Why do you suppose Dictionary.com chose to list them numerically as #1 and #2? It's because those parts of the definition best fit the most common way we're expected to understand the term.

Now, assign a value of either positive, negative, or neutral to each of the seven entries that define the term. I'd argue that each numerical entry within the definition is either neutral or positive with one exception. Entry #3 shows the possible definition going to an "excessive" level and resulting in "chauvinism."

What's the point of such a tedious dissection of this definition? I want to demonstrate just how difficult it is to take the term nationalism and twist it into something negative as so many on the political left did when President Trump described himself and his policies as those promoting nationalism.

As you can see, nationalism, by and large, is a positive or at least neutral concept. We know with relative certainty that President Trump understands it to mean the same. This is because he'd been asked to explain what it means to him multiple times on the record.

For example, in an article from *USA Today* on October 12, 2018, by William Cummings, titled: "'I Am a Nationalist': Trump's Embrace of Controversial Label Sparks Uproar," Trump is quoted explaining nationalism as "America first." He further explained, "I love our country, and our country has taken second fiddle." He further argued, "We're giving all of our money, all of our wealth, to other countries and then they don't treat us properly." Also, within the article, the author stated, "Trump said he was unaware the term carried any racist connotation and defended his use of the label."

With quotes such as those made both in public and on the record, one would think it would be difficult for any honest so-called journalist or talking head to confuse the meaning of President Trump's pitch for American nationalism. Right? Didn't he make it abundantly clear for inquiring minds to discern? Of course, he did. He even went further in explaining that his policies of nationalism are an effort to combat globalism and its harmful effects on America.

That didn't matter to the American left. They didn't allow a little thing like truth or accuracy get in the way of their dishonest narrative. We were instead treated to another example of the left redefining a term so that they could score political points and spread hate, discontent, and discord before projecting it back upon President Trump.

For example, CNN editor-at-large Chris Cillizza "penned" an article less than two weeks after the forementioned *USA Today* piece that theoretically painted a completely different picture. In Mr. Cillizza's article from October 23, 2018, titled "Donald Trump Used a Word He's 'Not Supposed To,' Here's Why," he also broke down both the definition and the use of the term nationalism.

Mr. Cillizza chose to use Merriam-Webster to define nationalism as

> a sense of national consciousness exalting one nation above all others and placing primary emphasis on promotion of its culture and interests as opposed to those of other nations or supranational groups.

Before going any further, I should clarify something about Mr. Cillizza purporting to use Merriam-Webster's definition of nationalism. First, he omitted Merriam-Webster's *very first entry* to define the term—that of "loyalty and devotion." Why on earth would he skip the very first entry within the definition of the term? He didn't even mention it. How would doing such a thing possibly help people to understand the concept of nationalism?

Next, Mr. Cillizza added what we must presume was his own twist to the definition as he explained without referencing any other entity what he called the difference between nationalism and patriotism. According to Mr. Cillizza,

> While patriotism, like nationalism, shares a pride and belief in one's own country or values, it doesn't include the idea of promoting your values and culture as inherently superior to those of others.

Mind you, that was not part of the Merriam-Webster definition (nor from Dictionary.com) yet Mr. Cillizza seems to purport it to be at least the primary if not only definition. This leaves us to suppose that this was fabricated by Mr. Cillizza under the guise of a definition by Merriam-Webster.

Mr. Cillizza also stated in his article "Words Matter," "...and, the American President referring to himself as a nationalist has all sorts of problems wrapped up in it." To that, I completely agree with the CNN editor-at-large. There are certainly problems with President Trump referring to himself as a nationalist. Sadly, the biggest problem is that we have dishonest propagandists like Mr. Cillizza lying and distorting the messages and policies coming from President Trump.

Mr. Cillizza inaccurately and dishonestly purported to use Merriam-Webster to define nationalism. He, then, chose to interject the one possible negative construct of the definition and linked it to a prevailing and historically European understanding of the term as it was applied to Adolph Hitler and the like. He suggested that as President

Trump was calling himself a nationalist, he knew that he was associating himself historically with Hitler.

The sad truth about Mr. Cillizza and his article is that Mr. Cillizza understood the importance of defining the term nationalism to his readers. It was his attempt to give credibility to his biased suppositions under the facade of fostering understanding and clarity.

He could have honestly and accurately defined the term (like I did), but he chose otherwise. Why? Because an accurate definition would only harm his phony narrative. Instead, he redefined the term so that it would mean something completely different and sinister. He then dishonestly associated the "new" definition (ironically, this example happens to be an "old world" or European definition) to President Trump.

Furthermore, Mr. Cillizza chose to omit all the recent quotes from President Trump in which he openly defined, clarified and further explained why he called himself a nationalist. This leaves us to conclude that for some reason, Mr. Cillizza didn't consider President Trump's *own words* recently uttered regarding the precise matter he was covering to be relevant.

I'll bet we can all guess as to why President Trump's own words were deemed as less than relevant to Mr. Cillizza. It's because Trump's quotes are the truth that invalidates the entire false premise of his piece. If you think that we should expect more from a CNN editor, you don't understand CNN and fake news.

Of course, the piece by Mr. Cillizza is simply one example among countless others that constituted the barrage of left-wing propaganda disguised as journalism or news specifically related to the redefining of the term, nationalism. This phony narrative led to the next related and unfounded charge aimed at President Trump, that of White nationalism, basically meaning White supremacy

Now, back to the question that introduced the chapter. When did the term nationalism (or nationalist) become a dirty word? Although it has had a negative connotation outside of the U.S. since about forever, the political left in America coalesced behind the negative construct when President Trump described himself as a nationalist.

Had President Obama publicly described himself as a nationalist, these same phony "hand wringing" critics would have been the first to provide to him any necessary political cover. Come on, you know it's true. Nationalism would have been "cool" and "hip." The phony Mr. Cillizza and his CNN cohorts would have been parroting, "It means patriotism. Look it up in the dictionary, dummy! This isn't Europe!"

But, rather, it was Trump that described himself as a nationalist. So, instead, the political left dishonestly redefined, demonized and politicized the concept. It's what they do.

10

Imperialism

Imperialism is a bit of a nuanced term. Like so many other words within our lexicon, it can have different meanings, sometimes significantly so. Remember, redefining America means taking the commonly understood meaning of a word or phrase and changing it to represent otherwise. And doing so to confuse or "game" the result primarily for political gain. Typically, this is done for no other reason than to demonize one side of an issue to poison and shut down any attempt at an honest and open debate. It's an overtly dishonest and destructive political strategy.

Merriam-Webster defines imperialism as a noun meaning:

1. The policy, practice, or advocacy of extending the power and dominion of a nation especially by direct territorial acquisitions or by gaining indirect control over the political or economic life of other areas. Broadly: The extension or imposition of power, authority, or influence. 2. Government, power, or authority: an imperial system.

As one can see, imperialism involves using power to take control of another nation or territory. When Merriam-Webster adds, "especially by direct territorial acquisition(s)," we know that to mean imperialism is typically understood as involving the "takeover" of territory or land that once belonged to another. What's meant by the "imposition of power?" When something is imposed upon another, it means that it did not involve a choice. This is a critical component in understanding the definition of the term.

Imperialism is *imposed or forced upon a person or people*. Under imperialism, there's no option to decline its imposition. There's no freedom to choose otherwise. Imperialism is antithetical to liberty and freedom. They're mutually exclusive. In other words, you can have one, but not the other.

What's our historical understanding of imperialism? Merriam-Webster goes on to discuss its historical usage and what they call its "linguistic roots." They involve colonialism and empire building. These concepts should conjure lessons from our schooling as young people. At one time or another, we all learned a good bit about colonialism and empire building and how it relates to the concept of imperialism.

In putting all this together, we get what I refer to as the commonly understood meaning of our term imperialism. Now, let's get into the politics of imperialism. Was imperialism as it was practiced throughout history inherently good or positive for mankind overall? No. It was a form of abuse and enslavement for those under the control of their captors. It was done for the sole purpose of using one group of people to enrich another. It was a blight on humanity.

Because imperialism was and is a terrible thing, anyone that would support or prescribe any form of imperialism be employed today would necessarily be a very bad person with very bad motives. Right? Under the universally understood definition of imperialism, anyone advocating for its implementation should be considered as supporting evil in our time. That's why the political left has also chosen this particular term to redefine.

The American left has redefined imperialism to promote their socialist ideology. They point to free trade between nations and regions and qualify it as imperialism. They choose to view two (or more) parties that *freely decide* to engage in the trade of goods, services, or monetary exchange for what each party considers as beneficial to them, as imperialism. Why?

Our friends on the left believe that capitalism is inherently evil. It's evil because it has people working for the motivation of profit. They consider a "for-profit" motivation as evil because it stands opposed to their socialist utopian belief of working for the collective good of all mankind.

In their effort to "sell" the masses on the merits of their chosen economic philosophy, the left wants to convince us that capitalism is evil. Their new definition of imperialism helps them to do just that. It works like this: when a poorer nation freely chooses to engage in trade with a richer nation (typically, the U. S.) for the betterment of both parties, the socialists among us are filled with righteous indignation.

"Look at the economic disparity between these two nations," they decry. "These (inherently greedy) rich people should be working for the betterment of the poor," they preach. "This is immoral," they spout. Then they work to sell Americans on the complete destruction of our economy through socialism in the name of what they consider morality and fairness. This typically comes from rich leftist hypocrites from the business, media and political classes that live in opulence rather than lowering themselves to living within their own belief system.

I began this chapter by describing imperialism as a nuanced term. Because the definition of the term also involves and includes "gaining indirect control over the political or economic life of other areas," the door is open, so to speak, for redefining the concept. At least, that seems to be the notion from the political left as they've taken this fragment of the definition to "spin" it.

Just as most good lies also have a fraction of truth, so, too, does the redefinition of imperialism. Under the new definition, having a certain degree of economic influence over another qualifies as imperialism. That's it. That's all it takes.

Under the new definition, no longer does imperialism require the acquisition of territory nor the imposition of power against the will of what would become the subjugated. Under this new definition, people all over the world freely choose to live under a so-called imperialist system and no one needs to be subjugated at all. The new definition of imperialism is simply living under the economic influence of others. And doesn't almost everyone do that to some degree?

In reality, the new definition of imperialism might seem pretty benign. Believe me, it's not. That's not how this works. Most Americans don't fully understand how this game is being played and perpetrated. For far too many people, the new definition of imperialism coming from the American left carries the same stigmatization as the old definition because nobody from the left cares to explain the difference.

You'll never hear from anyone on CNN or MSNBC nor read in the *New York Times* that freely choosing to engage in commerce most certainly does not fit the commonly understood definition of imperialism. Rather, they'll remain the soundboard for the deception. The term imperialism has been weaponized and is being used to fight for the cause of socialism. Now you know.

11

Disease

Now, here's a term that sounds innocuous enough. Some terms seem ripe for political manipulation while others seem more...harmless. Does the term "disease" strike you as an overtly political concept?

Merriam-Webster defines the term disease as a noun meaning,

> 1: a condition of the living plant or animal body or one of its parts that impairs normal functioning and is typically manifested by distinguishing signs and symptoms: Sickness, Malady.

They gave examples of "infectious disease" and "heart disease." They also have a second definition, "2: a harmful development (as in a social institution)." Their example of this is, "...sees the city's crime as a disease."

With this term, we see another example of more than one possible definition. However, as is so often the case, we have one true universally understood meaning. That would be definition number one. Again, there's a reason for Merriam-

Webster to choose to label a definition as its very first (dare I say, primary) definition.

Merriam-Webster's primary definition of disease has it ostensibly as a physical malady. At least, that's how it manifests itself. It's a physical ailment. That's how most everyone overwhelmingly understands the concept. That's how society understands and interprets the concept. That's also how many in the medical field define and describe a disease.

Definition number two is an entirely different conception. It's a political "can of worms." And definition number two is being used to conflate and converge the understanding of the term for political gain. Allow me to explain.

I came upon an online article on a site, verywellhealth. com, that helps clarify the meaning of what's medically considered a disease. According to the article, "a disease is a pathological process that healthcare providers are able to see, touch, and measure." It's "distinct and measurable." The article is titled "What is the Difference Between a Disease and a Disorder," written by Cory Martin and medically reviewed by Scott Zashin, M. D. I chose to use this article because the author endeavored to do just as I'm attempting to do. He defined, described, and clarified like terms that are often confused. As he clearly stated, a disease is distinct, tangible, and measurable.

This article is relevant because it demonstrates what we find from the purveyors of information that are interested in science versus politics. This is an example of an article that truly seeks to clarify and coalesce a greater understanding of terms and concepts. It's an honest piece, free of politics and the dishonest phony narratives that accompany so many partisan pieces.

Now, let's look at what we get when we mix science with politics. When I typed the terms "violence" and "disease" into the search engine Bing, the very first entry that was presented to me was a workshop summary from The University of Illinois at Chicago, by Gary Slutkin, M.D., titled "Violence is a Contagious Disease." According to Dr. Slutkin, "violence, meets the definition of a disease and of being contagious." Isn't that interesting? I wonder if someone would be willing to inform this doctor that violence doesn't remotely fit the definition used by folks like verywellhealth.com, nor does it fit the universally understood definition used by most Americans.

Don't discount the fact that this study was the first "match" from the Bing search engine. If you don't believe that algorithms are used by "big tech" to promote a political agenda, you're naive. This is a big part of the politics of the American left. This study came up first by design. The "wizard behind the curtain" made sure that we saw this article before anything else might otherwise affect our ability to "educate" ourselves.

This was only one such example of the politicization of the concept of a disease. There are countless other examples dating back decades in which violence is purported to qualify as a disease. This redefining of a disease isn't new. The Centers for Disease Control and Prevention (CDC) had taken to this notion of treating violence as a disease since the early 1980s. They even established their Violence Epidemiology Branch back in 1983.

Don't get me wrong. I'm not suggesting that those working to promote violence as a disease are inherently corrupt or deceitful. I'm sure many of them are righteous people with good intentions. However, politics generally involves corruption and deception. So, what other corrupting factions and factors are also involved in redefining a disease to include concepts such as violence?

An article from Chicago Health, titled "Healing Society's Soul," gives us a look into some of the history and politics of this matter. As one might expect, government funding and research into "root causes" become a point of both motivation and contention. According to the article,

In 1996, the National Rifle Association (NRA)

was waging war against Congress and the Centers for Disease Control and Prevention (CDC).

That war started three years earlier in 1993, when CDC-funded research led to a study published in the *New England Journal of Medicine*. In "Gun Ownership as a Risk Factor for Homicide in the Home," researchers made a strong correlation between firearms in the home and an increased risk of homicide.

As a result of subsequent pressure from NRA lobbyists, Congress stripped the CDC of $2.6 million for gun violence research and passed the Dickey amendment, which states that "none of the funds made available for injury prevention and control at the Centers for Disease Control and Prevention may be used to advocate or promote gun control."

The American Psychological Association condemned the amendment at the time. In 2015, Doctors for America, the American Academy of Pediatrics and other medical associations asked Congress to repeal it.

Former President Barack Obama also made that futile request after the Newtown massacre at Sandy Hook Elementary School in 2012. A few years later, a gunman opened fire in a nightclub in Orlando and, again, nothing changed politically.

What am I getting at here? I think we can all see the political motivations behind redefining the term disease. The political motivations include acquiring money (government funding), pandering to constituencies (for votes), coalition building, dispensing of funds (and the power it affords) and more. Adding in the altruistic reasons related to a "general benefit to society" and you come up with all sorts of driving forces to redefine the concept of a disease.

I don't consider it too tangential to also refer to what's become of science and the role of medicine in recent years. As everyone knows, COVID-19 was used as the rationale to lock down otherwise free people and to subjugate our rights and liberty. This was a measure never seen before in the history of America. So-called leaders in the field of medicine, including the CDC, were given power by proxy like we've never seen. To many of us, this was unimaginable power and outside constitutionality.

Understanding what we experienced by living through this, do we really want to empower these unelected bureaucrats even more by allowing them to redefine terms that could or would expand their purview over our lives under the auspices of science and medicine? Hasn't everyone witnessed enough of the floundering Dr. Fauci flip-flopping and contradicting himself as he created dictates from "on high?" Was that the will of "we the people"?

Science and politics are a terrifying combination. Redefining terms such as disease enabling the misuse of science to promote and justify the bestowing of unconstitutional powers to politicians and bureaucrats cannot continue to happen. We simply cannot allow our political class to misuse science to promote or even worse to once again forcibly mandate an extreme political agenda.

12

Gender & Gender Affirming Care

Thanks to the political left in America, the concept of gender has become one of the most heavily debated issues of our time. Gender is defined by Merriam-Webster as, "a: Sex," and "b: the behavioral, cultural or psychological traits typically associated with one sex."

Then, they go into the newer 21st Century definition of "gender identity." According to Merriam-Webster, "gender identity refers to a person's internal sense of being male, female, some combination of male and female, or neither male nor female."

Again, we have a term that had a universally understood definition based in science and physiology. It was generally understood that a man has male chromosomes and male body parts while a woman has female chromosomes and female body parts. Just a short time ago, this was not a matter for debate. This was pretty darn near a matter of fact. This definition worked just fine for nearly all of America as well as the rest of humanity for a very, very long time.

Not anymore. We have a sizable contingency primarily from the political left that insists on taking a factual, science-based definition and adding the concept of *feelings* to it. Why was this necessary? As you likely know, it's being done for inclusiveness. It's being done because it allegedly makes some people feel better about themselves.

What's wrong with making people feel better? On its face, nothing. In a vacuum, nothing. However, we don't live in a vacuum. We live in the real world with real world implications related to a "fluid" definition that doesn't match reality.

I'll let Temple University Professor Heath Fogg Davis, a proponent of the new definition of gender, help explain why this redefining is important and necessary for leftists. In an article posted on what's called *Temple Now*, titled "How the Gender Identity Revolution Impacts Society," Professor Davis suggests that this redefining and all that comes with it is a matter of respect and understanding of others that are different than the norm. That's all. He's just asking for some respect and understanding for people that are different. Really? We'll get back to the musings of Dr. Davis shortly.

But first, I'd like to interject with an opinion of my own. You can play around with pronouns all you like. It's a free country. If you really want to go around spouting, "he, him" and "she, her" nonsense verbiage to try to make some people feel good about themselves, go right ahead. I'm not going to try to stop you. I'm a pro-freedom kind of guy.

Unfortunately, there's more to it than that. As we've learned throughout previous chapters, the American left is loath to leaving any Americans the right to think and act freely. Rather, we must conform to them and their "enlightened" ways of thinking, "or else." For example, there's anti-discrimination law and transgender civil rights to consider. In other words, it just may be illegal to believe otherwise and act upon it. Be careful. You had better get with the leftist program. You may be outright breaking the law and subject to legal recourse. I'll get back to that shortly.

Let's return to the so-called teachings of Professor Davis at Temple University. Do you think you're going to make it through Temple or anywhere else in academia these days without surrendering your core beliefs to that of the radical left? According to Temple University's Professor Davis, he'd like to see "...fewer gender markers used in a public sphere because there is such great potential for getting it wrong. When we get it wrong, it can inflict a lot of harm..."

Evidently, you have to go to school for a very long time and become an enlightened leftist to fully understand the gravity of what we're dealing with as a society. All of America and perhaps the entire world must change the way we refer to and speak with people that are confused about their gender, or else bad things can happen. And just what kind of bad things might happen? As the professor professed, "it can inflict a lot of harm." A lot of precisely what kind of harm is the professor warning us about here?

Brace yourself. Are you sitting down? Someone might get *"embarrassed."* Really!

Hey, I'm not looking to embarrass anyone, nor to embarrass myself. American society needs more civility and empathy. I'm quite sure many would agree that 21st century America in the age of the internet is sorely lacking in both civility and empathy, among other things. But that doesn't readily come through coercion, force, and silencing others that disagree.

Now, let's look at some actual harm and real damage coming from this movement and what leftists consider enlightenment. We now have schools that are hiding their "treatment" of children that they believe may be misgendered from the parents of the children. With a few extreme exceptions, *schools do not have authority over parents in determining what's best for their child.* Again, schools are hiding so-called treatment from parents.

We now have many examples of children on puberty blockers that will forever alter these children's bodies. We have leftists telling biological men that they're women and biological women that they're men. Is this really helping them? We have biological men competing with women in women's sports. We have men in women's locker rooms. That's a problem. Little girls need to be protected from this environment. This is disgusting.

From Yahoo News, in an article titled "Teen Girl Blasts YMCA Trans Policy after Encountering Naked Man in Women's Locker Room," from January 2023, we get a better understanding of the harm being done by these radical policies. According to the article:

> A female minor is speaking out against the YMCA's transgender inclusion policy after she encountered a naked man while showering in the women's locker room at a San Diego location. 17-year-old Rebecca Phillips was showering at the Santee facility after her swim workout when she noticed a naked man in the women's locker room. Miss Phillips also used the phrase "child endangerment" as she considered the possibility of having her 5-year-old sister exposed to the same scenario.

Do you think Temple University Professor Davis and his cohorts consider and discuss child endangerment as they sell their ideology? Me neither.

Another sad reality and result of this twisted psychology can be understood through the anecdotes of individuals that were child patients placed on powerful hormone drugs with side effects that are irreversible. Warning: you can easily find articles from what seem to be reputable sources that claim puberty blockers and hormone treatments are completely reversible. In some cases, this is true. However, by and large, it is not. These treatments have been proven to have lifelong consequences. They cause sterility and stunted height. According to many of the so-called experts, side-effects include a significant loss in bone density, greater risk of cancer and cardio-vascular disease as well as psychosis.

This doesn't even take into account the cases of children having body parts surgically removed or altered.

There's a contingency of leftists that are selling us on the notion of having our children make gender-related decisions themselves. *Children cannot provide informed consent regarding these life altering decisions.* How is this even debatable? They're children. Isn't this elementary (no pun intended)?

Fortunately, thanks to the political left in America, everyone can feel good about their gender now. And, feeling good about yourself is what being an American liberal is all about. Again, the mixing of science and politics is a very bad elixir. The politics of feelings has no place in biology or science. Beware of those promoting such a combination and do not trust their motives.

Are these professors and teachers truly educators as they proclaim? Are these political advocates of so-called "gender rights" really looking out for the best interest of our kids and society as a whole? Or is this just another example of the political left redefining a term or concept for political purposes with little concern for common sense and the resulting calamity?

GENDER AFFIRMING CARE: What does it mean to "affirm" something? Dictionary.com defines the term affirm as a verb meaning, "1. to state or assert positively; maintain as true." And "2. to confirm or ratify." Putting this together, we get a term that positively confirms something to be true and/or factual.

Now, what does the term "care" mean? Well, it can mean a host of different things. However, in this case, we're looking for what Merriam-Webster calls an idiomatic phrase, "take care of," meaning, "to attend to or provide for the needs, operation, or treatment of (someone or something)."

Putting it all together, a definition making use of the universally understood meaning of all three terms combined (using "sex" from the previous chapter to define the term "gender") would give us *treatment to provide needed confirmation of one's sex.*

Tell me (rhetorically, in case I'm not within "earshot"), does corroborating with someone, *especially a child*, the notion that they're whichever gender they choose to be qualify as "gender affirming care?" I'll rephrase the question. Does telling someone that they are whatever gender they feel like "affirm" a gender?

No. It does exactly the opposite. It clouds any possible affirmation. It then becomes hard to argue that one is providing *care*, don't you think? Rather than helping one to understand and comprehend their actual physical gender, we have so-called healthcare providers telling confused people that they are whatever they think they are or perhaps want to be.

Allow me to clarify something. As a conservative-libertarian, I strongly believe that any American adult has the right to whatever type of health related "care" they desire. If you're at the age of consent and want to pay someone to mutilate your own body, go right ahead. It's ultimately your choice and a decision you'll have to live with. I honestly hope it makes you happy. Believe it or not, I am empathetic. Although I don't understand the plight, I feel bad for these gender-confused people. What they put themselves through is a hell of a choice.

Here's where things get contentious. To those on the political left promoting cultural poison disguised as help and concern, *stay away from the kids*. Their minds aren't developed yet. They're learning, maturing, and growing. Leave them the hell alone.

How about some commonsense logic to which most of us can relate? If your child isn't mature enough to eat whatever they want, sleep whenever they want, dress however they want, handle their own hygiene, drive a car, get tattoos, check into a hotel room, own a firearm, do their own banking, date whomever they want, and move into their "partner's shack," *then they aren't old enough to choose genital mutilation and puberty blockers.*

Also, as Americans living in the land of the free, if someone chooses to go through surgeries and other medical procedures, they should pay their own related bills or find someone to help. American taxpayers are not responsible for surgical or other procedures designed to make people happy. We don't collectively pay for "boob jobs" or "hair plugs." American taxpayers are getting "soaked" for enough nonsense. Pay for your own procedures that are strictly designed to make you feel better about yourself.

I remember listening to Dr. Sebastian Gorka on a radio show that I cannot recollect well enough to cite nor directly quote. What I do remember from his interview as it related to this subject matter was his contention that the mutilation of genitals is not "care." Yet, it's sold to us as healthcare by the American left.

He also stated that a psychiatrist doesn't affirm a psychosis...doesn't order a 75-pound bulimic to purge after meals because she believes that she's too fat. Nor would anyone support a patient that believes he's Napoleon by affirming such a delusion. I support Dr. Gorka's assertion that the left supports what constitutes a "gender psychosis" for political and ideological reasons.

Remember, the American left has "cornered the market" on kindhearted qualities such as compassion, understanding, equality, love, and tolerance. At least, that's their contention. And to a leftist, feeling good about themselves and how they affect culture is the pinnacle of existence. That's how they can myopically claim to be the champions of the misunderstood misgendered members of society.

The leftist political class and punditry use the politically driven leftists in academia to give credentialed certitude to their disingenuous notion that promoting a leftist ideology amounts to higher education and a greater level of understanding. We've seen this in earlier chapters within this book and we'll see more examples going forward.

They hold a myopic view of the world as they readily

choose to ignore the obvious damage they leave in their wake when "successfully" implementing their leftist policies. To the left, any negative consequences to their dogmatic policies are either ignored or explained away as somehow necessary to reach a level of overall betterment to society.

This is how and why we find ourselves fighting against the political left and their redefining of terms such as gender, care, and so many others.

13
Woman

Ready for a hot one? This has been widely debated and emotionally charged for quite a few years now. What's a "woman?" Both Merriam-Webster and Dictionary.com define the term woman to mean, "an adult female person." When defining "female," they both get a little "murky" with longer explanations involving the ability to produce eggs, and the use of what they consider as synonyms, "gender" and "gender identity." The bottom line is, if you're an American beyond the age of adolescence, you've spent your life understanding the term woman as referring to one's biological makeup.

Until recent times, one's biology, meaning basically one's chromosomes and body parts, placed you into a category of either a woman or a man. Let's call that the science of it. The American left likes to use science as the authority or point of adjudication (when convenient) to determine what constitutes truth in matters of debate. Well, let me rephrase that. The American left like to use science as such in cases providing it helps their side of the debate.

For example, according to leading Democrats, you couldn't challenge the COVID-19 government mandates precisely because doing so was allegedly counter to science. "Follow the science," was both a command and a reprimand from the left as it was (mis)applied to all things COVID-19 related. However, following the science isn't as convenient when applied to other subjects such as assigned gender (or killing babies, or race and racism, or...I digress). It's important to understand the rather obvious hypocrisy from the left to further understand their motives.

What has the political left done to redefine what it means to be a woman and for what purpose? As an example, let's look at an article from *Time* magazine, in March of 2020, titled "What Does It Mean to Be a Woman? It's Complicated" by Susan Stryker. In her (wait! Can we call her a "her?" Or... *crap!* I let them do it to me again!)

In the opening paragraph, she gets right to it. She writes:

> Only the delusional would deny biological differences between people, but only the uninformed can maintain that what the body means, and how it relates to social category, doesn't vary between cultures and over time.

OK. You know what comes next. Let's break that down a bit. According to the author, and by extension *Time* magazine, it would be delusional not to consider biology. At least she was able to recognize the obvious. That's good. But, as we're told by the author, it's really complicated. That's because we also need to consider what the body means, how it relates to social category, and how it relates to cultures over time. What the hell does that even mean?! And my favorite line from the quote—*only the uninformed would disagree with her*. Feel free to research this article and read it in context. It reads like nonsense to me. But maybe that's the idea. Remember, it's *complicated*. That's a primary point within the article. I'll get back to that shortly.

The author goes on:

> Those willing to recognize new forms of gender feel

anxious about misgendering others, while those who claim superior access to the truth are prepared to impose that truth upon those who disagree.

This single sentence is like "liberal gold" (my quote, not hers). If you want to understand the mind of a leftist, this is a "right proper" case to study. *Wow.*

It's beyond implied by Ms. Stryker that those finding agreement with her philosophical doctrine can recognize and achieve a new level of understanding. You see, as is so very common with the political left, they've "progressed" and grown to a new level of understanding beyond that of their protagonists. That's how they view themselves and those that agree with their understanding of the world around them.

Likewise, they stake claim to the moral high ground because their beliefs are rooted in care and consideration for the grievance group that they're so anxious to appease rather than offend. And to her detractors, by evidence of any disagreement to willingly redefine what it means to be a woman, shame on you for your self-righteousness and intolerance.

According to Ms. Stryker, those that don't agree with the new and enlightened definition of woman (falsely) claim superior access to the truth and impose their intolerant and intellectually inferior version of truth on those that disagree. Do you see how she and the other previously quoted leftists portray themselves as the enlightened good guys and those that disagree with them as the "knuckle-dragging" bad guys?

What's perhaps more problematic is that she seems to be demanding that the rest of us change our (uninformed) ways to no longer be intolerant of others. The gist of her point is that she and others that agree with her are simply right and those in opposition are simply wrong because the forces on the political left simply understand things better. Therefore, those that disagree *must change*. Does the notion "I'm right and you're wrong, therefore you must change" represent tolerance? Or perhaps instead it represents hypocrisy on the part of Ms. Stryker.

I'm going to make a suggestion: if you find yourself debating an issue and your argument ends with the suggestion—no, the *demand*—that everyone who disagrees with you must ultimately change their ignorant ways, do yourself a favor and steer clear of the concept of intolerance. Leveling a charge of intolerance while simultaneously practicing it yourself will not strengthen your argument.

There's still an important component to Time magazine's example of redefining the term, woman. It's regarding precisely who it is that's doing the redefining. Below the article (online) was the following: *"Stryker is a presidential fellow and visiting professor of women's, gender and sexuality studies at Yale University."*

Isn't it interesting to know that this line of thinking has gotten this person a fellowship and professorship position at such an "elite" institution as Yale University as well as publication in Time magazine?

There's a reason I feel the need to use quotes to surround the word elite in this case. It's because there's nothing "elite" about this line of thinking. It doesn't really qualify as deep thinking at all, in my opinion. This is the same old, tired tactic and sales pitch from the political left. You're supposed to be impressed, however, by the credentials of the author.

We've seen this before. The credentials of these authors suggest that they're scholarly intellectuals. Therefore, don't we need to give greater credence to the content of the piece? That's the idea. Because the political left controls academia in America, they can grant to one another the gift of advanced degrees, fancy titles, awards, and other accolades for their diatribes supporting leftist beliefs that have come to be known in academia as "intellectual" and "scholarly" works. It's really just a big circle jerk.

I'll finish this chapter with one more thought. Remember the title of the preceding article? Again, it was, "What Does It Mean to Be a Woman? It's Complicated." Do you know *why* it's supposed to be deemed (and "sold" to us) as complicated?

It's because a simpleton such as you or I can't be expected to understand it. It's too darn complex and nuanced.

The rest of us aren't equipped for such an intellectual feat. We need to leave that to the "gifted" among us. We need to leave the burden of comprehension to the "smart people." We need to follow their lead and "do as we're told." After all, who are you? Where's your fellowship? Where's your professorship? What's your title and from where was it earned? Yale? Harvard? What's your requisite pedigree, pal? These so-called educators and institutions of higher learning teach bias and in some cases hatred as an equivalent to higher learning and intellectual thought.

As my favorite radio and television show pundit, Andrew Wilkow, likes to say, "Your academic pedigree doesn't outweigh the strength of my argument." Remember that, folks.

14

Gain of Function

T his chapter is going to begin a little differently. As you know, we typically refer to "good old" Merriam-Webster or Dictionary.com to define relevant terms and/or phrases. After all, how can one discuss the act of redefining terms and phrases without having an original definition as a starting point?

"Gain-of-function" is a phrase that has a meaning in the world of science and that, since the dawn of the COVID-19 pandemic, has been politicized. And as I've stated repeatedly, science and politics are a very bad elixir.

Where does one go to find an unbiased and non-politicized working definition of gain-of-function? I settled on a site called Phys.org due to several factors. It's rated as non-biased by 3 sources I came across while researching efficacy (Media Bias/Fact Check, AllSides, and Quora). The site is purported to be pro-science with both high credibility and high traffic. Also, it's based in the United Kingdom rather than the United States. I prefer to use a reference source outside of the U. S. in the hope that it should be less likely to be influenced by American politics.

According to Phys.org, gain-of-function has a very generic meaning in which an organism acquires a new ability or property to gain a function. According to the site, "This can happen through natural selection or a researcher's experiments. Some of these methods involve directly making changes at the level of genetic code."

As they work their way more towards the relevant matter of this chapter, they state:

> In the current debate around SARS-CoV-2, the virus that causes COVID-19, gain of function has a much narrower meaning related to a virus becoming easier to move between humans, or becoming more lethal in humans.

Despite foremost efforts by some in the realms of science, media, and politics to obscure the truth and "muddy the waters," one doesn't have to have doctoral credentials to understand the issue. We had a genetically altered, SARS-related virus (from the Wuhan Institute of Virology in China) that gained the ability to "jump" from animal to human, spread globally from human to human at a high rate of infection, and with a significant lethality rate. The research that was being done at the Wuhan virology lab did, indeed, meet the universally understood definition of gain-of-function research.

The choice to include gain-of-function as a redefined concept for this book goes "against the grain" a little bit. Other terms and concepts from other chapters are more commonly understood with a more conventional definition. The primary reason I chose to include gain-of-function is because it helps to illustrate the real-world ramifications of redefining terms. We've all been witness to how this contrived strategy has been implemented and its effect regarding gain-of-function.

Dr. Anthony Fauci, immunologist and Director of the National Institute of Allergy and Infectious Disease (NIAID), among other titles and roles over the years, showed us how it's done. To refrain from chasing down Dr. Fauci-related "rabbit holes" such as his lies and self-contradictions, false predictions, funding sources, and political bedfellows (for the most part), we're going to focus squarely on the effect of having Dr. Fauci create his own definition of gain of function.

As America and the rest of the world began to learn more about the origins of the COVID-19 pandemic, Dr. Fauci was exposed for his role in the funding of the Wuhan virology lab with American tax dollars. One of the many problems with this revelation is that in 2014 the U. S. federal government placed a "pause" on U.S. funding of gain-of-function research. And in late 2017, the moratorium was lifted for "naturally occurring pathogens that are circulating in or have been recovered from nature." That order came via the U. S. Department of Health and Human Services.

To make a long story short, Dr. Fauci, along with other collaborators in high places, are responsible for directing all sorts of American funding to the Wuhan lab post 2017. Did they commit any crimes or improprieties? According to Dr. Fauci and others, no, they did not.

That's because, again, according to Dr. Fauci and others, no American funding went directly towards gain-of-function research. Other so-called experts in the field disagree entirely. They're on the record stating unequivocally that what was done by Dr. Fauci and company certainly did constitute gain-of-function research.

So, what's the truth? Money and politics have clouded the issue. Half of the partisan divide doesn't want an answer. The other half is still fighting to get one. Personally, the Wuhan funding argument reminds me of past debates on abortion funding in which liberal Democrats were insisting that using tax dollars to support clinics that provide abortion services isn't the funding of abortion, itself.

That's because according to the clinics, no tax dollars went directly to the actual physical abortion service. Get it? It's kind of like, "I put that money in my right pocket; not my left pocket." Or the disheveled, hungry-looking stranger asking for a hand-out for food takes your charitable donation into the store and comes out with a sandwich and a bottle of liquor while insisting, "Don't worry, I used *your* money for the sandwich." Is there a difference? Really?

Here's the point of the chapter: As long as Dr. Fauci and company are able to define or perhaps redefine what they were funding and researching as something other than gain-of-function, they're largely in the clear. Remember, it was illegal for them to direct U. S. funding to this kind of research. Furthermore, Dr. Fauci also testified under oath to congress that his work did not include gain-of-function research. The very definition of gain-of-function stands to determine the possible criminality of his actions and subsequent (false) testimony. That can't be understated.

Does this case help in comprehending the gravity of what can result from redefining our language? In cases such as this, it can be the difference between innocent or guilty in a court of law. It can be the difference between honest testimony and perjury in a Senate hearing. It can be the difference between the exoneration of a public figure in a position of trust versus moral and ethical turpitude.

This sort of political, legal, moral, and/or ethical dichotomy is the by-product of redefining terms in America and elsewhere. The act of redefining terms and phrases is being done consciously to confuse and to manipulate. It's being done deliberately to alter what's factually wrong into what's right or vice versa. And it's being used to debase our legal system to misrepresent truth versus lies. It's a very big deal.

It's the reason and the purpose of this book.

15

Insurrection vs. Riot

W e've all been treated to the rather recent politicization of the concepts of both "riots" and "insurrection." Many Americans sat at their domiciles during the COVID-19 "lockdowns" and witnessed via television the reports of hundreds of riots primarily throughout 2020 and into 2021. Needless to say, the less fortunate among us experienced these deplorable acts and events up close and personally. Sadly, some people lost their lives. Riots seemingly became the norm in some parts of America.

What's a riot? Merriam-Webster defines riot as a noun meaning "a violent public disorder. Specifically: a tumultuous disturbance of the public peace by three or more persons assembled together and acting with a common intent." That about covers it. Simply put, some people got "pissed off" and collectively tore things up. That's the nature of a riot.

Now, how does that differ from an insurrection? Merriam-Webster defines the term insurrection as a noun meaning, "An act or instance of revolting against civil authority or an established government." This is where things get a little trickier. The U. S. Federal Government further qualifies and criminalizes it as, 18 U.S.C. (Code) 2383.

Let's go to Cornell Law School for further clarification of the U. S. Federal Government's definition of insurrection:

> Whoever incites, sets on foot, assists, or engages in any rebellion or insurrection against the authority of the United States or the laws thereof, or gives aid or comfort thereto, shall be fined under this title or imprisoned not more than ten years, or both; and shall be incapable of holding any office under the United States.

An important distinction is that an insurrection includes a specific aim to take over or undermine the government, whereas a riot does not. That's the difference. Conceptually, it's not difficult to understand. However, as is often the case, to judge one's intentions as a rioter versus insurrectionist can become more opaque.

For example, when four far-leftist Antifa members burned down a police station during a so-called protest in Minneapolis in May of 2020, was that an act of insurrection? Was it "An act or instance of revolting against civil authority or an established government"? It kind of seems so. But they were charged and consequently pleaded guilty to one count each of conspiracy to commit arson. I recall nobody describing them as insurrectionists, nor did I read any such suggestion upon my research for this chapter of the book.

How about when, in March of 2021, Antifa members set fire to the federal courthouse in Portland, Oregon? Does targeting the Federal Courthouse constitute a "rebellion or insurrection against the authority of the United States or the laws thereof?" Weren't their actions specifically aimed at undermining part of the government? Didn't their actions fit Merriam-Webster's definition, "revolting against civil authority and an established government?"

One certainly could have made that argument. Yet, who did? They were deemed to be rioters almost universally, except for leftist mouthpieces that described the scene as "mostly peaceful." Do you recall anyone describing these actions or these actors as insurrection or insurrectionists? Me neither.

Can anyone forget CHAZ (Capitol Hill Autonomous Zone) or, as it later became known as, CHOP (Capitol Hill Organized Protest)? What about Occupy Wall Street a decade earlier? These so-called protesters took over entire blocks of a major American city and violently clashed with police as they tried to maintain civil order and enforce the law. Were these so-called protesters engaging in an insurrection?

Honestly, even these extreme cases don't fit neatly into the insurrection category. However, they're arguably the closest examples we've seen of insurrection in modern times. They "check the most boxes." They're examples that are probably as near to insurrection as anyone alive today has ever seen or experienced in America. Despite this being the case, nobody was charged federally with 18 U.S. Code 2383.

Not only did we not have legal indictments of insurrection for perpetrators linked to CHAZ/CHOP and Occupy Wall Street or Antifa, the other "perps" of relentless violent street crime (remember over 100 straight nights of riots in the summer of 2020?), but were these criminals even publicly described as insurrectionists? No, they weren't.

Not only were they not considered as insurrectionists, many left-wing so-called journalists wouldn't even describe these perpetrators as rioters. Instead, we were treated to video footage of looters robbing and burning businesses often actively fighting with law enforcement while a leftist with a press pass described the scene as "mostly peaceful" and the rioters as "protesters."

Let's not forget about the Democrat office holders at different levels and locales parroting the same lying narrative. They were "mostly peaceful protests" by people that have a "right to be angry." That's what we were told. "Nothing to see here," as cities literally burned.

What's the difference between an insurrection versus a

riot versus a protest? To the political left, it's politics. Given the evidence of the past several years, politics is the ultimate qualifier.

All the rioters from CHOP/CHAZ, Occupy Wall Street, Antifa, and BLM were (are) radical leftists. All the criminals within these groups are leftist activists. Therefore, they're "well-intentioned" and "misunderstood." That's what the political left in America told us for years. That was their phony narrative.

Riots were becoming almost the norm especially throughout 2020. Again, we had over 100 straight nights of riots in just Portland alone. According to the National Police Association, there were 574 violent riots within that calendar year, resulting in over 2,000 injured police officers and literally countless other injuries. I recall hearing reports of property damage totaling over a billion dollars collectively. Again, this was in just one year, the worst year, 2020.

If you recall, these riots, or mostly peaceful protests, were "understandable." According to the political left, the real villains were racist police officers (even non-White officers were considered White supremacists). And the real problem was systemic racism and inequity within the entire justice system and institutional racism and inequity throughout pretty much the rest of America. Man, that's a lot of racism and inequity! I almost burned down my own home just thinking about it! This is what you call left-wing logic.

Then, everything changed.

On January 6, 2021, we saw a paradigm shift. We had what looked like a riot by angry members from, this time, the political right. They were Trump supporters that showed up at the nation's capital primarily to protest the handling of the 2020 Presidential election. Then, the violence broke out.

This was unacceptable! It was a disturbance unlike we had previously seen. Remember, violence and destruction had almost become the norm. What happened on January 6 was different, we were told. But why?

Did it last longer? No. It was over in a few hours unlike the previous riots. Was it the level of damage and destruction? No, that was very minimal in comparison to the riots by the political left. Was it the level of physical injuries or loss of life? No. Again, that was also very minimal versus the countless riots that preceded it.

The difference was the rioters and their grievances. You see, all the other riots were political leftists and Democrat constituencies tearing the country apart in the name of left-wing causes. They were good people with understandable rage because life isn't fair and America is a racist nation, according to the political left.

Although the level of violence and criminal acts on January 6 were but a tiny fraction of what we saw from the Democrat-supported riots, these rioters from the right side of the political spectrum were prosecuted to the maximum extent of the law. After all, these were Trump supporters. They were evil people committing evil deeds. They were going to pay dearly. The Justice Department under Democrat control set out to find every single one of them! And it seems they did.

The January 6 riots were a "threat to Democracy" we were told. We "nearly lost or republic." They were an "insurrection." I couldn't begin to cite those quotes, as they seemed to come from every leftist and "anti-Trumper" every day. They were uttered literally countless times by countless Democrats.

So, why did the three-to-four-hour long riot with little to no coordinated plan and almost no weaponry resulting in minimal damage on January 6 constitute an insurrection? And, conversely, why did the seemingly unending riots with destruction to property totaling over a billion dollars and injuries to more than 2,000 police officers, and on and on, only amount to "mostly peaceful protests?"

We all know why. *Politics.*

On January 6, 2021, the Democrats and the rest of the political left redefined the concept of an insurrection. A riot in the nation's capital in support of a political conservative and in protest of an election is now considered an insurrection, according to the political left.

Interestingly, although the perpetrators from the January 6 riots and President Trump had been convicted of insurrection in the court of public opinion by the Democrats, Trump-hating Republicans, most of the media, and the rest of the leftist cabal, it's important to note that *not one person has been charged with insurrection.* (U.S.C. 2383). You know why? It's because no court would find any of them guilty of insurrection. *That's because there was no insurrection.*

There were other crimes committed. But not insurrection. One would otherwise have to redefine the term. Sadly, we were all witness to that monumental and undeniable effort done in the name of Democrat and anti-Trump politics.

16

Book Banning & "Don't Say Gay"

The subject of "book banning" became a "front page" point of debate across the entire nation as Governor DeSantis worked to sign into law Florida's Parental Rights in Education Act in 2022. As I'm sure you remember, it was more widely known by its nickname crafted by the American left, the "Don't Say Gay" bill (and subsequent law).

For the record, the Florida law forbids "classroom instruction" on gender identity and sexual orientation for children from kindergarten through third grade. The idea, needless to say, was to maintain age-appropriate classroom learning. Its design is to try to keep agenda-driven interests from trying to influence children that are too young for matters of a sexual nature. The American left has described that endeavor as hate, bigotry, and censorship.

In an effort to persuade fellow Americans and win the debate over legally codifying such a thing as age-appropriate sex education in the classroom, the political left began asserting that their conservative rivals were banning books.

What does it mean to be banning books? We all know what books are. So, what does it mean to "ban" books? Banning is defined by Merriam-Webster as "to prohibit, especially by legal means." Also, "to prohibit the use, performance, or distribution of..." Thus, we get books that are illegal to own or distribute. That's what it truly means to ban books.

Is that what happened in Florida? Is that happening elsewhere? Are books being banned around America?

According to Reader's Digest author Elizabeth Yuko in an article titled "What Is Book Banning, and How Does It Affect Society?", book banning has a different definition. The author allegedly went to the American Library Association (ALA) for their definition. What we got was:

> Book banning is the act of removing materials from a school or library's collection as a result of objections from groups or individuals who say that they need to protect others—typically children—from the difficult information or ideas contained in the books.

How about that? We got a new and politically convenient variation of the definition. In other words, the phrase was redefined.

This is one example of how *keeping age-inappropriate books from little children* was being referred to as book banning and the cultivation of such a premise. Now, if organizations such as the American Library Association (ALA) say it, it must be true. Right?

To be fair to the ALA, they were almost certainly referring to banning books specifically from school libraries, not from the whole of society. Here's the rub, the Readers Digest writer (conveniently) failed to make that discernment. Rather, she informed us that, "The United States has a long history of book banning," and "This form of censorship began...in the 17th century and never went away." Within her article, she promoted the dishonest notion that age-appropriateness equates to the government telling citizens what they can and can't think and believe. As if kindergarteners through third graders represent the whole of the United States. This is another example of what leftists do to twist, manipulate, and redefine the meaning of words and phrases to promote their chosen agenda.

In Florida, we witnessed an entire bill (that became law) unofficially renamed by the American left. It was done in a similar manner for the same reasons as other attempts are made to redefine commonly understood terms. Despite truth and reality, the Parental Rights in Education Bill/Law is better known as "Don't Say Gay."

The point of this chapter is simple: *Keeping classroom instruction age appropriate is not book banning.* Nothing has been banned. All the ceremoniously approved garbage being promoted by the political left in America is still available to just about anyone. It just isn't going to be in grade school libraries or school curriculum for children below fourth grade in places like Florida. Again, it's simply a matter of being age-appropriate. Wasn't this considered common sense just a short time ago? This is not a new or unique concept.

Ultimately, this is just another example of the political left in America fearful of an honest debate. They know that they can't win popular support with the truth. They can't win the narrative with the message that left wing so-called educators should control sexual content for kindergarten through third grade children and that parents' rights don't matter. They don't want to have to answer for why they shove pornographic materials, sometimes gay and "trans," to children as young as kindergarten.

Seriously, have you ever heard anyone ask these creeps, "Why do you *want* to do this?!" This is sickening. Why don't we have Democrat leaders being held to answer why they support having pornography, gay or straight, "taught" to little children?

I'll tell you the answer. It's because when asked, they say that they're against book banning and government censorship. In other words, they lie. They redefined book banning to create a figurative strawman and phony narrative. They falsely draw an equivalence to age appropriateness and book banning/censorship. Then, they refuse to answer the actual questions related to promoting their perversion.

Instead, they suggest that they're fighting conservatives that want to ban books and censor Americans. Again, it's a lie. But with the help of their enablers in the media, academia, and the leftist political class, it works to keep them from having to stand in support of the indefensible.

This is what redefining book banning (and censorship) has done for the American left. Rather than having to defend supporting "porn for kids," they can stand opposed to banning and censorship. As is typical, their true agenda is a loser and their lies are more effective as they successfully redefine book banning in the minds of many Americans.

America, be wary. This is what's happening to our society and to the most vulnerable among us, our children. It's sick and twisted. It's the American left at work manipulating our culture through our children.

17

Far Right/Conservatism

I f you've spent any amount of time watching, reading, or listening to "mainstream" media sources, you've certainly been exposed to the American left and others redefining of conservatives and the "far-right" political faction in America. Merriam-Webster defines the far-right to be a noun meaning "The group of people whose political views are the most conservative." That's certainly inarguable.

Political conscrvatives constitute the righl side of our spectrum while American liberals (the antithesis of classic liberals) and/or progressives are found on the left. This is elementary. But what constitutes far right vs far left values and visions? We need a more comprehensive understanding.

For this, I went to Dictionary.com. They were willing to delve deeper into the meaning of this phrase and wade into its social and political aspects by asking the question, why? More specifically, Dictionary.com asked and answered the question, "Why Do 'Left' and 'Right' Mean Liberal and Conservative?"

They go on to define for us what left and right mean:

In politics, the word left is applied to people and groups that have liberal views. That generally means that they support progressive reforms, especially those seeking greater social and economic equality.

Dictionary.com seems to promote the notion that seeking social and economic equality makes you a leftist. As if *only* leftists seek economic equality. That's a load of garbage! They go on with:

The term far left is often used to refer to those who are considered to have more extreme, revolutionary views, such as those who espouse communism and socialism.

Now, following this progression of logic and understanding, we have people called leftists that are simply seeking greater social and economic equality. This sounds good; sounds noble. As is so often the case, who wouldn't support *that* definition and understanding of what it means to be a leftist?

What happens when we take leftism to its end? What, again, are "far" leftists? They're socialists and communists! Am I the only one that's having trouble understanding what seems to be a monumental disconnect? We took a group of people, leftists, that went from noble, caring types primarily seeking equality, to commies and socialists when left unchecked by their political foes.

Those leftists that are graciously described as simply those seeking social and economic equality are aligned or categorized with communists and socialists. They're fighting together for the same cause(s) and against the same political adversaries, the political right.

Back to Dictionary.com and their defining of "the political right":

The word right, in contrast, refers to people or groups that have conservative views. That generally means that they are disposed to preserving existing conditions and institutions. Or they want to restore traditional ones and limit change.

I'll add that the conditions and institutions that the political right are commonly fighting to preserve and restore are primarily constitutional ones. I'm referring to the U.S. Constitution, the guarantor of liberty in America.

According to Dictionary.com, "The term far right is often used for more extreme, nationalistic viewpoints including fascism and some oppressive ideologies." This is certainly the leftist approved definition and how the far-right are most often described. Is it accurate and true? Let's parse this definition.

We're to believe that the political right in America is working to preserve and restore traditional institutions and limit change sharing a kinship with the far right as they fight for...fascism?! Again, they're suggesting that constitutionalists on the political right that are fighting for social norms and traditions are in league with far-right *facists?*

Oh yeah, and don't forget about the "oppressive ideologies." They're referring to nationalism. And as we covered in an earlier chapter, they're referring to the more global/European definition of nationalism, meaning chauvinism and racism.

Remember, President Trump, representing conservatives, calls himself a nationalist while clearly explaining that he means "America first" and patriotism. At the same time, leftist Democrats tell everyone that he really means that he's a White supremacist. It's a political strategy that's dishonest, destructive, and hateful, but it works for them.

Let's get back to right vs left ideology and apply logic, coherence and some sorely needed realism. How do our definitions of left and far left meet with reality here, in 21st Century America? For example, who are American leftists and what do they prescribe?

They had a leading candidate for President, Bernie Sanders, that's a "dyed-in-the-wool" socialist. Bernie represents a leading "face" of the Democrat Party. What about the "squad" members? They and countless other Democrats support measures such as defunding the police, wealth redistribution, the revocation of gun rights, racial quotas, riots without consequence for leftist causes (only), and the removal of ballot safeguards to protect the integrity of elections, just to name a few.

Do these sorts of causes fit the Dictionary.com definition of left or far left? Absolutely, they do. They espouse views that are revolutionary and extreme in comparison to traditional American values. Contemporary Democrats are at least friendly to socialism while some are advocating for it, outright. And they do this under the guise of social and economic equality. Their definition of the political left and far left, indeed, fits 21st century reality. It fits the far left "like a glove."

What about their working definition of right and far right? How do these definitions meet with reality? The first thing that jumps out at me is that, as Dictionary.com suggests, the actors on the political right are in a nearly endless battle to stop the left's persistent attempts at wholesale change or what they consider reform. Regardless of whether one favors any such changes or not, it's telling. It depicts one side more often as the change agent leaving the other side fighting for what they consider a proper normalcy. Oftentimes this does, indeed, meet with reality. Not always, but certainly often enough, this fits what Dictionary.com describes as the political right.

Now, what about the Dictionary.com definition of far right? This is where things get convoluted at the very least. Let's start with academia. Here's a jewel of an example of how the "educated" among us are "teaching" the rest of us how to understand these matters.

Psychology Today had a study from a survey in 2019 titled: "Why People Support Far-Right Political Views." The objective of the survey was to determine which participants would be classified as authoritarian and/or socially dominant.

The author of the study defined "socially dominant" as one that prefers "social inequality" (versus equality). This so-called study involved a survey of 410 participants that were described as, "mostly American citizens of White/European ethnicity."

The survey was done to determine whether the participant shows characteristics that fit within four designated classifications: "prejudice," "social dominance," "right-wing authoritarianism," and/or "far-right support." Let's see how the study determined individual participants to be loathsome enough to fit among the author's classifications. You're going to love this.

According to *Psychology Today*, if you agree with the participants that believe "Discrimination against blacks is no longer a problem in the United States," then you're prejudiced. You aren't deemed as someone that disagrees with convention. You aren't incorrect or misinformed. You aren't a person with differing experiences. What you are is racially prejudiced. Isn't that the same as being racist?

Sadly, I'm just getting started. According to the survey, to be classified as socially dominant, one must believe that "An ideal society requires some groups to be on top and others to be on the bottom." Are you of the opinion that those individuals that typically make good life choices will find themselves "on top" versus those that consistently make poor life decisions? If so, according to *Psychology Today*, you openly stand for social inequality. Damn you.

If you believe that "Obedience and respect for authority are the most important virtues children should learn," you would fit the classification of right-wing authoritarian. I truly had no idea that teaching such virtues to children was the determining factor for such a moniker and such a sign of social malignancy.

Finally, we get to what the study considered as far-right support. Perhaps you guessed it. If not, you shouldn't be surprised. According to the study, if you support President Trump, you're a far-right supporter. There's no middle ground. There's no gray area. If, given the choices within our two-party system, you chose Trump over Hillary, Biden, or Kamala, you're a supporter of the far-right. What if you "plugged your nose" while choosing? I guess it doesn't matter.

Why should we care about what *Psychology Today* is promoting? Everyone should care when people that purport to represent academia and science choose, instead, to promote dishonest politics. Just as redefining commonly understood terms and phrases is being done specifically to confuse and manipulate the masses, *Psychology Today* does likewise.

They're pretending to be a science-based and research-oriented entity that exists to promote a better understanding of the human mind. The preceding article and so-called study that they chose to publish under their name was nothing but leftist political propaganda. It was packaged as scientific research to sell to the masses and help redefine what it means to be ideologically aligned with the political right (or far-right).

Under the auspices of gaining a greater understanding of the science of the human mind, they dishonestly (and clumsily, wouldn't you agree?) demonized their political foes. *Science!* Sure, it is.

I'd like to conclude this chapter with some thoughts on the concept of authoritarianism. The political left considers and "sells" the narrative that conservatives represent the far-right. There's nothing conservative about authoritarianism. As previously stated, conservatives believe in the preservation of traditional values and norms. Our values and norms have been codified throughout the history of our republic by our elected representatives. Our republican form of government is the complete antithesis of authoritarianism.

The left's embrace of socialism and communism, however, is not antithetical to authoritarianism. Quite the opposite is true. Socialism and communism *require* an authoritarian form of government. This holds especially true if a nation were to transition from the inherent liberty of a representative form of government to that of socialism and communism as so many leaders of the American left prescribe.

Once again, according to Dictionary.com: "The term far left is often used to refer to those who are considered to have more extreme, revolutionary views, such as those who espouse communism and socialism."

Let's add fascism, progressivism, and any other leftist approved "ism" you choose to include. What's the link between all of these leftist promoted "ism's?" They all involve the erosion and subversion of individual liberty for the leftist's desired form of collectivism imposed upon the citizenry by force of government.

The political left is working tirelessly for change. Their vision for America is the social and economic "equality" a nation gets by turning from free market economics to collectivism. Socialism, communism, fascism, progressivism, and the like are all forms of collectivism. Such a form of government requires centralized planning to manage the people and the system. Who are the prescribed planners that would manage or control the system? Naturally, the planners would be the leftists, the so-called visionaries. And finally, what do we call a system that's managed and controlled by central planners? It's called an *authoritarian* system.

As we can all see, the political left in America has conveniently redefined what it means to be right and far right versus left and far left. They use every tool at their disposal to reinforce the false narrative. We're all used to the cabal of politicians, media pundits, entertainers, and so-called experts helping the political left to sell their lies.

I believe that America is still "waking up" to the realization that science and academia are being falsely used to corroborate and validate these lies as factual, then to classify and archive these lies within curriculum to be formally taught primarily to young people. It's really no wonder so many Americans believe they live in a nation on the decline. In so many ways, the left has won the day.

18

Fascism/Authoritarism

"President Trump and his supporters are fascists! If you disagree, you're a fascist." That's the sentiment we've been hearing from the political left for years. That was the political left's (focus group-tested, I'm sure) mantra leading up to the 2024 Presidential election. That's also what we hear from a group that call themselves "Anti-fascists" or "Antifa."

What is fascism? According to Merriam-Webster, it means:

> a political philosophy, movement, or regime...that exalts nation and often race above the individual and that stands for a centralized autocratic government headed by a dictatorial leader, severe economic and social regimentation, and forcible suppression of opposition.

This is their first and most detailed definition. Their second definition sort of sums things up a bit: "a tendency toward or actual exercise of strong autocratic or dictatorial control."

As is typical, the first definition is the best. As I contend, that's precisely why it's the *first* one. What's great about this definition is that not only does it inform us as to what the concept of fascism encompasses and promotes, it also delves into the reasoning as to why.

Fascists believe, in part, that the needs of the nation as a whole should be put above the needs of the individual. As is always the case with a form of government that places the perceived good of the citizenry (as a collective) over that of the individual, there needs to be an authoritarian leader (or leaders) as the central planner that controls the levers of power. We've covered this theme before in other chapters. It's comparable to socialism in these regards.

Fascism, like socialism, is antithetical to the U.S. Constitution and its underpinnings of the guaranteed protection of individual liberty and what's supposed to be an open and free market-based economy. Fascism, in theory, adds to socialism a dictatorial leader that suppresses opposition by force and typically the existence of a racial superiority component.

Now, let's delve into how the American left is selling the concept of fascism in the modern era of politics. The political left in America, also known as 21st Century Democrats, have been largely supportive (tacitly, at the very least) of the ideology behind the group Antifa. They've been on the record on countless occasions making excuses and justifications for the group's actions and "protecting them" from law enforcement and the justice system. Since around 2016, they've also been selling America on the notion that President Trump and his supporters are modern-day fascists.

In this chapter we're going to dig into the narrative, "Trump's a fascist." Then we'll move on to the concept of authoritarianism. We'll finish with a discussion of Antifa.

Do you remember former U.S. Secretary of Labor (under President Clinton) and current professor of public policy at U.C. Berkeley Robert Reich? He wants to help us. He had an article in *The Guardian* titled "Trump and the Republican Party exemplify these five elements of fascism" that articulates the argument for the political left. Let's look at each of these elements.

The first element, according to Reich, is "The rejection of Democracy, the rule of law and equal rights under the law in favor of a strongman who interprets the popular will." His points of evidence are the following quotes from Trump: "The election was stolen" and "I am your justice...I am your retribution."

The first quote has been uttered by many a failed candidate and campaign from both parties, just as Hillary Clinton did after losing to Trump in 2016. I couldn't even begin to list all the failed candidates from any political party that shared that sentiment.

President Trump tried and failed to use *the law* to support his claim of a broken and unconstitutional election. He didn't use the military or a threat of force. He used a team of lawyers. Whether you agreed with his case and tactics or not, that was President Trump making use of the rule of law. Ultimately, he lost and has since disagreed with the rulings. However, his challenge was done through the political and legal system.

"But, but January 6...!" To avoid chasing down a January 6 rabbit hole and instead staying on topic, I'll just posit this: The Democrats and Trump-hating Republicans that supported the shameful, phony, mock "insurrection" trial didn't even have enough evidence to bring such charges against him in an actual court of law. Why wouldn't the same people that changed the standard for impeachment and impeached him twice without any hope of conviction then worked to have him charged with over ninety crimes primarily designed to damage him politically, not even charge him with what they assured us was insurrection?

They *had to* have a phony impeachment trial because an actual trial would have involved the process of "discovery" and would have allowed Trump to face his accusers and mount a defense. This would have ended in humiliation for Liz Cheney, Adam Kinzinger, and the Democrats.

Mr. Reich's second quote was intended to demonstrate authoritarianism. However, he gave no examples of any authoritarian actions or policies. To accuse Trump of authoritarianism because of innocuous words on the "stump" or elsewhere without any examples of dictatorial action despite holding office for four years, is a hollow and empty point.

Let's do better than Mr. Reich. Let's look at some legitimate examples that genuinely fit his first element of fascism. Does impeaching and voting to remove a duly elected President twice having not met the established standards of proving bribery, treason, or high crimes and misdemeanors fit the element of rejecting democracy and the rule of law?

How about a President that was denied the right to face his accusers and/or mount a defense during impeachment hearings? How about using lawfare against a candidate to keep him in a courtroom, wasting time and hemorrhaging resources in the hope of locking him up in prison? What about attempting to have someone removed from the ballot that's winning in the polls? How about ignoring our border law? Or ignoring the Supreme Court's rejection of "forgiving" student loans?

Leftist Democrats did these things. I could go on and on. These actions by Democrats most certainly reject democracy and distort the rule of law.

The second element is "The galvanizing of popular rage against cultural elites." Mr. Reich used these Trump quotes as examples: "Your enemies are media elites...the elites who led us from one financial and foreign policy disaster to another." Mr. Reich suggests that fascists "galvanize public rage...stir up grievances...use mass rage to gain and maintain power."

Forget Trump—nobody stirs up grievances like the Democrat party, especially at the national level. The foundation of Democrat politics is to categorize and divide every American into their assigned grievance group based on race, gender, ideology, economics, religion, and anything else imaginable for the abject purpose of ginning-up rage against their political foes.

Democrats have been implementing this political strategy for decades, tearing our country apart purposely. How about the burning, beatings, looting, and more from the radical left that defined the summer of 2020? Again, this is projection and the height of hypocrisy.

The third element is, "Nationalism based on a dominant 'superior' race and historic bloodlines." President Trump's quotes include, "Tremendous infectious disease is pouring across the border." This is a shameless example of racism on the part of none other than Mr. Reich, himself. Injecting race and racism into subject matter *that has nothing to do with race* for political gain is inherently a dishonest and racist political tactic.

If Mr. Reich and the rest of the Democrats had evidence of actual racism by President Trump, they wouldn't have to fabricate it. They'd be able to simply cite actual examples of truly racist quotes. But they don't because they can't. Rather, we get volumes of anecdotes from Democrats claiming, "This is what Trump said, but here's what he really meant..." Again, this is inherently dishonest and can be "done to" or "said about" absolutely anyone to slander them.

Another Trump quote Reich used was, "Getting critical race theory out of our schools is ... a matter of national survival." This is another sickening example of Mr. Reich's own racism. Critical race theory, the theory that everyone is either a victim or an oppressor based on race, is inherently a racist, dishonest, and horribly divisive theory. For Mr. Reich to label President Trump a racist for simply not buying into this theory is both pernicious and corrupt.

Think about it—these were the best examples of so-called racism that Mr. Reich found to cite in support of his article and its premises. Evidently, he could do no better.

It's hard to believe that a so-called educator publicly labeled the President of the United States a racist for not believing a theory on racism that divides children in the classroom into non-White victims versus White oppressors.

I happen to agree with President Trump. Am I a racist, according to Mr. Reich? Are you as well? Yes, according to Mr. Reich and many leading Democrats, if you don't agree with their radical, divisive, and hate-inciting politics, it's simply because you're racist. According to Democrats, disagreement equates to racism. "Choose love, not hate," they say as they foment hateful sentiment purposefully for the sake of politics.

The fourth element is "Extolling brute strength and heroic warriors." Trump's quotes that allegedly demonstrate fascism are, "You'll never take back our country with weakness, you'll have to show strength and you have to be strong" and "I am your warrior." Again, these are innocuous quotes that could have come from many different political leaders at any time in our nation's history. And these quotes are what Mr. Reich and *The Guardian* use as evidence of fascism. How sad and weak is this argument?

Finally, as this gets a bit tedious, we get to the fifth and final element of fascism, "Disdain of women and fear of non-standard gender identities or sexual orientation." This is just comical! The "great minds" on the left can't even define what it means to be a woman, and I seriously doubt Mr. Reich would have the courage to show off his intellect and help us out with this important distinction.

Now, think back to your history lessons and the occasion when fascist regimes such as that of Mussolini were studied. Do you remember learning about the objectionable treatment of non-standard gender identities by fascists? Me neither. What the hell is he talking about? Isn't it obvious that he or one of his cohorts simply fabricated this crap to pander to a constituency group? Where's the historical relevance between fascism and the concept of gender identity? He and his cohorts just made it up.

We can easily guess why Mr. Reich presented no such evidence. All this gender-related nonsense is just the "flavor of the week" or the subject "du jour" designed to make leftist politicians and academics appear intellectual, fashionable, current, and of course, compassionate. Truth be damned.

Mr. Reich and his leftist friends are helping the rest of the political left to redefine what it means to be a fascist. This is being done so that President Trump and his supporters can be successfully labeled as fascists. That's the purpose of redefining the concept of fascism (Yes, I finally got to the point of the chapter, hooray!).

As an aside, this is what the Democrat-controlled left considers intellectual discourse from one of their distinguished "thinkers." Aren't you impressed? This man, Reich, is not an educator. He's a hypocrite and an impostor. He's a cheap salesman. Sorry, I mean sales*person*. I wouldn't want to offend members of non-standard gender identities or sexual orientations.

This is an example of the cabal that is leftist politics meeting with so-called higher education and giving credence and approval by "respected journals" such as *The Guardian*. Aren't you impressed by their credentials? They hope so, because the merit, the honesty, and the strength of their arguments shouldn't impress anyone.

Let's look at some real-life examples that better fit the actual meaning of fascism and/or authoritarianism. On the theoretical level, conservatives are the constitutionalists among us waging a constant battle with the political left and their promotion of a "living, breathing" U. S. Constitution, evolving with time and leftist political will.

Which side of the political aisle better fits Mr. Reich's first element of fascism, "rejection of Democracy...the rule of law?" Conservatives are the ones most often fighting *for* the rule of law as it was originally intended and crafted through the democratic process (within our republic).

The political right typically fights to preserve the law while the left fights to manipulate it. This phenomenon is primarily how a large faction on the political right became known as conservatives. Theoretically, this is what it means to be a conservative. Conservatives want to conserve the status quo. In this case, the status quo would be the rule of law and the U.S. Constitution (as it was written and intended).

Which party has members threatening to "pack the courts"? For decades Democrat officeholders have been appointing activist judges and justices to legislate from the bench, undermining the democratic process rather than interpreting the law as it was written and intended. Recently, since President Trump's successful appointments to the Supreme Court, Democrats have also been threatening to pack the Supreme Court with more activist justices. These actions and threats of action are certainly examples of the rejection of democracy and the rule of law.

What does it mean to be "authoritarian"? According to Dictionary.com, it's an adjective meaning: "favoring complete obedience or subjection to authority as opposed to individual liberty." Politically speaking, authoritarians favor a system of government in which freedom and individual liberty are subordinate to the power of government.

Authoritarians believe that they can better manage the lives of Americans than can the citizens themselves. And in some places, they're attempting to prove it. For example, in New York City, residents are banned from owning or acquiring natural gas-powered stoves, gasoline-powered cars, wood-fired pizza ovens, and large-sized sodas, among other things, as legislators work to include bans on salt and detergent pods. The State of New York has banned pet stores from selling dogs, cats, and rabbits. Who runs New York City and the State of New York? It's leftist Democrats, the thieves of liberty.

The Biden Administration imposed federal COVID-19 vaccine mandates. Many were overturned through litigation prompting many others to be withdrawn. President Obama worked to outlaw the incandescent light bulb in 2007, only to see President Trump roll back the ban in 2019. Now, President Biden has outlawed them again. They were doing this while calling President Trump an authoritarian when they weren't labeling him as fascist.

Political factions primarily from the political right

have been fighting the left for freedom from a litany of authoritarian measures all over America. Examples are the fight against the vaccine mandates and mask mandates. Conservative Republicans are fighting for choices in health care (versus socialized medicine), school choice, ending confiscatory and punitive taxes, and ending our border crisis. They're stopping so-called global warming initiatives, so-called entitlements, and Democratic socialism. They support free markets, fair elections (with election day, not election month), second-amendment rights, and, in the case of actual conservatives (not RINO's and Republican globalists), combatting our debt crisis.

Conservatives are fighting for our freedom against Democratic authoritarianism and socialism. President Trump and conservative Republicans are fighting the Democrat left in America against countless authoritarian measures.

ON ANTIFA: What is Antifa? According to Dictionary.com, Antifa is:

> a political movement whose followers are left-wing activists who oppose fascist authoritarianism, capitalism, and extreme right-wing ideologies such as nationalism, xenophobia, and White supremacy.

OK, now, what does all that mean? There's no question that they're left-wing activists. I can't imagine anyone disputes that initial characterization. Friends, foes, and members alike should agree that they represent a far-left ideology.

Although I don't love Wikipedia, they had a broad and well detailed description of Antifa. Members include, "anarchists, communists, socialists," and they "describe themselves as revolutionaries." They may achieve their aims through "non-violent direct action, incivility, and violence." People who identify as Antifa members "use tactics involving digital activism, doxing, harassment, physical violence, and property damage." Other than that, I'm sure they're fine folks. If this description is accurate, and we all know that it is, these people largely represent *violent criminals*.

As an aside, isn't it interesting that Dictionary.com chose such a "sanitized" definition for Antifa at the time of my inquiry? They made no mention of how they're objectively known for their violence and destruction bestowed upon anyone with which they disagree. As Wikipedia notes, that's the essence of who and what they are. They're far leftists, anti-capitalists, socialists, and communists. Yet, they purport to be against fascism and authoritarianism. Here's a news flash for the hopelessly confused: You can't have socialism or communism without an authoritarian system of government.

Socialism and communism *require* a centralized system with someone controlling the levers of power. The central planner(s), the person or people placed in position(s) of control over the management of the system (formulating rules/laws, creating divisions of labor, providing for the needs of the masses, etc.), are called *authoritarians*. They represent governmental *authority*. You Antifa people are very confused.

Let's not forget their most noble of causes. Antifa is fighting against nationalism, xenophobia, and White supremacy (allegedly, emanating from the political right). As we covered in the chapter on nationalism, there are numerous definitions of nationalism. Antifa isn't against the most commonly understood definition in America, that being patriotism and a sense of national pride. Patriotism was President Trump's definition of nationalism and the same definition that I and many others were formally taught in school. They're against nationalism as defined to mean chauvinism or racial (White) supremacy.

So, they want to fight against Neo-Nazi skinheads. Who the hell doesn't? Who, on the political right, supports White supremacists? I can think of nobody. Unless, of course, we allow leftists to redefine racism and White supremacy to include anyone that doesn't agree with their radical agenda and won't concede to their (twisted) political will.

We ended slavery in America more than 150 years ago. We don't have Jim Crow or apartheid in America either. As a matter of fact, every American, regardless of race, lives under a legal, political, and economic system that treats them the same as anyone else. At least that's the objective.

We strive for the best form of equality we can have. The political right believes in equality of opportunity. Do you know what the far-left calls equality of opportunity? They call it racism.

The political left in America believes in equality of outcome versus equality of opportunity. To the left, it works like this: you count the number of members within a business or any organization. If the number of so-called minorities isn't proportional to (or greater than) the total population in America, it's racist. That's what they consider institutional racism. Here's the beauty of it for the radical left: *It's never going to be proportional.*

That's virtually impossible as long as we have something in America called choice or free will and consequences to behavior. What leftists in America hate to acknowledge is that we live in a certain reality. In the real world, the choices one makes in life have a direct impact on their success or failure. Sane people would have things no other way. The far left, however, disagrees. They want an equal outcome for everyone regardless of choices and behavior. Try to get them to even acknowledge and discuss how behavior affects outcome in life. Go ahead. Try. But be prepared to be demonized as a practicing racist.

This is how and why the radical left supports various forms of socialism. Socialism is the leftist's notion of equality and the apparatus for its enforcement. Always remember, it's so wonderful that it has to be imposed upon the citizenry by force of government. But just like leftists don't like to acknowledge that one's behavior is the key to success versus failure in America, they also don't like to discuss their vision of trading away our liberty for socialism by force of government. Certainly, there's no other way to implement such a decree. Even if socialism is enacted through a democratic process, it's maintained against dissent by force, typically the barrel end of a gun.

It's fine for Americans to disagree on the politics of sociology, economics, biology, theology, etc. As a matter of fact, it's downright American to do so. What's not acceptable is to lie, demonize, and even to bring violence and destruction upon others for having the temerity to disagree. That's the "gift" from Antifa to the rest of America.

As we've seen time and time again, the political left demonizes those who disagree with their vision for America. They can't just disagree. Rarely do they challenge ideas with logic and fact. Rarely do they even attempt to persuade, debate, and win people over to their way of thinking, as Americans have typically done for two and a half centuries. Rather, they use the politics of division and hate. If you disagree with an American liberal, you're "racist," or "sexist," or "homophobic," or "greedy," or "bigoted" or "fascist." But aren't we used to that by now? Sure. We're used to that sort of verbal venom. That's been the norm for decades.

What we aren't accustomed to in America is the use of outright violence by members of a political faction. The radical left now has their "brown-shirts" committing physical acts of violence and destruction on their behalf. That's who and what Antifa is. Black Lives Matter works in similar fashion. Now, the American left has an army that can fight for them literally, not just metaphorically.

If you're not so sure about the collusion between the political elites on the left and the violence of Antifa, let's further make the connection. Here's an example from the *New York Post* by Jason Rantz, from January 2021, titled "Democrats Are Now Paying The Price For Empowering Antifa:"

Portland militants rioted for more than 100 consecutive

nights, yet...District Attorney Mike Schmidt declined to prosecute some 70 percent of cases. He justified his position by acknowledging that he agreed with the activists' anger. When Antifa showed up to harass Mayor Ted Wheeler at his home, the mayor said he'd move, quite literally allowing the thugs to chase him from his own home.

And:

In Seattle, Mayor Jenny Durkin ceded a piece of her city to militants to create the region's original autonomous zone. She then stayed silent for months as activists tried to murder police, even cementing shut a door to a precinct while trying to set fire to a building. The city council rewarded such actions by defunding the police.

Many Democrats allowed Antifa atrocities because they were committed by fellow leftists fighting for the same causes. And of course, because they share a common political adversary. Many Democrats have "sold their souls" to Antifa believing that the perceived political gains justifies the violence and destruction. "Stand down" orders to police from Democrat leaders for Antifa rioters looting and destroying businesses, burning private property, and terrorizing citizenry is the essence of support. Antifa members are violent authoritarians claiming to be against authoritarianism. They're a living, breathing, walking, fighting, burning, beating, and vandalizing hypocrisy fighting both for and against their own mission statement.

It's interesting that Robert Reich's descriptions of the five elements of fascism fit Antifa quite well. Not the rather idiotic irrelevant nonsense about "disdain of women and fear of non-standard gender identities." Or the absurdity of fighting against the political right to defeat White supremacy. I'm referring to the elements that accurately describe and define fascism: *"The rejection of Democracy and the rule of law. The galvanizing of popular rage against cultural elites. Extolling brute strength and heroic warriors."*

When we combine these elements with relevant parts of the actual definition of fascism, we get Antifa. In other words, as we break down the definition and characteristics of fascism and compare them with the actions of Antifa, we get a match. Antifa (the self-proclaimed Anti-fascists) are, indeed, modern-day fascists.

As an aside: The term "Nazi" is short for "Nationalsozialist," which literally translates from German to "National Socialist" Party. Think about that when the Democrat left are calling conservative Republicans Nazis while espousing the virtues of socialism. Think about that when Democrat leaders are calling Republican members of the House Freedom Caucus the far right and linking them with Hitler and White nationalism.

Nazis were socialists (among other things) fighting for authoritarian government control (the antithesis of freedom and liberty). Likewise, socialist Democrats in America are fighting for authoritarian control and against conservatives, the defenders of our freedom and liberty.

19

Violence

I suppose it's fitting to have the chapter covering the concept of "violence" immediately following the spotlight on Antifa. According to Merriam-Webster, violence is defined as: "The use of physical force so as to injure, abuse, damage or destroy," and "an instance of violent treatment or procedure." These were both entries within Merriam-Webster's first definition. There were three additional definitions as well, but this is certainly the universally understood definition of violence.

What's important to understand about violence is that it's a *physical act*. It's the use of physical force with the intent to do harm. It can also be a treatment or procedure as well, albeit a malicious one (see Nazi Dr. Josef Mengele performing medical experiments at Auschwitz during World War II). The key point is that it's a physical act (or acts) with bad intentions.

By now, you may be wondering, what has the political left done to hijack the concept of violence? Let me tell you. In case you haven't heard, according to the left, words are now violence. Yes, words. You know how this works. We'll need to investigate how and why.

I felt it reasonable to look at Reason.com to learn more. In an article from July 2020, titled "In 2020, Words are 'Violence,' Arson Is Not," we get right to the crux of it. According to the author:

> The leftist case for redefining "violence" relies on two main arguments: damaging a person is morally more serious than damaging an object, and psychologically damaging a person is worse than physically damaging an object.

Let's "unpack" this.

I like that the author went right to the fact that it's, indeed, the political left redefining our term. We should appreciate the reinforcement, necessary or not. The author also quoted several leftist activists and supporters of riots, including one Nikole Hannah-Jones from the 1619 Project. Regarding the first argument, that of "people vs objects," she says that "it's not moral" to draw an equivalence between destroying property and doing physical harm to a person. Therefore, she contends that, "Destroying property, which can be replaced, is not violence."

So, there we have part of it, the so-called logic. Let's call this the leftist philosophy that allows them to absolve themselves from the sin of perpetrating violent acts involving the destruction of property. To these leftists, it's only property. It's no big deal, I guess. One can replace "things." That's the argument. How very juvenile, wouldn't you agree?

Does a business that someone worked half of their lifetime to build qualify as simply a replaceable object? Does the means to feed a family, pay a mortgage, or afford a retirement qualify as replaceable objects? What about when someone chooses to defend their property? I don't remember the radical leftist rioters dancing to any such pacifistic tones of this woman, Nicole from the 1619 Project, that cares so deeply about the immorality of physically harming people (versus objects). This is utter nonsense. This so-called philosophy doesn't meet with reality.

But wait, it gets far worse. Don't forget her second main argument for redefining violence, "psychologically damaging a person is worse than physically damaging an object." If you thought the first so-called argument was off base, this one is really obtuse.

What does it mean to psychologically damage a person? It's precisely what it seems to mean. To these radical leftists, it's no big deal to be rioting in our streets, burning, looting, vandalizing, and terrorizing communities because these like-minded leftists are just doing harm to objects. But don't you dare damage their psyche by disagreeing with them, criticizing them, or even questioning their methods! That's doing real harm to a real person. That's real violence! So, they say.

How about some examples? Within the same Reason. com article, there were several real-life examples cited. In Baltimore, resisting to help change city policy by replacing the word "sex" with "gender identity" was deemed as, "violence against the transgender community." Not properly referring to Black people in America as African Americans is a lack of nuance that is violence. And according to BLM, "White silence is violence."

The summary within the article articulates the rioters' perspective reasonably well:

> To review: not speaking is violence; speaking charitably but clumsily is violence; having an unpopular opinion or providing a platform for one is violence; insisting that both parties honor legally binding contracts is violence; burning buildings, smashing windows, and destroying businesses is not violence.

Another very important facet to this mind-numbing affront to both logic and reality is this: radical leftist rioters and their supporters are using what they call "violent words" aimed at them (due to their own behavior) to justify their violent physical acts. Following this line of thought, if you say something that these petulant snowflakes choose to find offensive, you have perpetrated violence against them. Your hurtful words are considered as violence towards them. And what's the justifiable response to someone that initiates violence towards another person?

Think about this from a legal perspective. If someone brings violence upon someone else, what becomes legal recourse? Let me try asking this question in another way. If you witness some poor radical leftist Democrat fire-bombing someone's storefront but otherwise minding their own business and you tell this person that they simply cannot behave in such a manner, you will likely offend that leftist. If your words are construed as violence towards these rioting leftists, then you may have just brought violence upon that rioter. When violence is initiated against someone, they have the legal right to use violence in return as a matter of self-defense.

You don't believe me? If words equate to violence, this is certainly true. Do you trust our modern-day justice system? Do you really doubt that this sort of example could become an actual legal indictment of a high-profile conservative Republican in a deep blue state or municipality?

We all need to wake up to the lawfare being waged in America today. We have leftist judges and justices fabricating their own versions of law. We have district attorneys refusing to prosecute criminals for violating laws that don't fit their political orthodoxy while simultaneously selectively prosecuting political adversaries. Our legal system is in disarray from leftist office holders at the local, state, and federal levels using lawfare as a weapon.

Our language is being manipulated so that the citizenry can be manipulated. Then, when words have different meanings, our systems can be manipulated such as our legal system.

When or if we allow the political left in America to redefine what constitutes violence, just imagine what terror awaits us in the future. If we give in to the violent radicals doing the bidding of the political left and allow them to control the streets, the leftist riots from the summer of 2020 may become the norm in America.

Think about all the harm and destruction we experienced when the radical left went unchecked. Try to imagine calculating a toll that considers all of the physical injury, property damage, and emotional harm done by the radical leftist mob to date. Consider a future that would leave them empowered to bring upon America more of the same kind of mayhem.

20

Progressive

The general inference regarding the term "progressive" certainly leads one to believe that it would involve "progress." After all, isn't that the root word within the term, progressive? Merriam-Webster defines it first as an adjective, then a noun. Their first and most understood definition is "of, relating to, or characterized by progress." There's nothing new there. Right?

It's when defined as a noun that the term progressive takes on another meaning. Merriam-Webster defines progressive as a noun meaning "one believing in moderate political change and especially social improvement by governmental action." Here's where things get interesting.

What better describes and encapsulates the entire "modus operandi" of the political left than the second part of Merriam-Webster's definition, *"social improvement by governmental action?"* Interestingly, even diametrically opposed actors from both sides of the political spectrum can agree that those from the left promote an agenda that involves using governmental forces to affect social change. That's what I love about Merriam-Webster's formal definitions of this term. What I'm sure the political left loves about these definitions is that they can claim to fit their ideology within both definitions of the term.

Most American leftists claim to promote moderate political change. Remember, to the left, their viewpoints rarely fit the description of radical or extreme. But do self-proclaimed progressives really promote a moderate form of change?

For example, as many leftists were fighting for a governmental takeover of the healthcare industry in America (a "single-payer system"), how was it described by the plan's supporters? To the political left, a change in healthcare so profound that it would redefine the entire relationship between the citizen and government wasn't considered as extreme or radical.

To the left, taking the ability to make medical decisions, up to and including life or death treatment, from patients and doctors to a system based on governmental approval is just good sound policy. To the American left, giving the federal government the power to deny healthcare service to citizens, turning citizens into subjects, promotes equity, fairness, and progressive values. They perceive any form of socialized medicine as progress.

The part of the formal definition of the term progressive describing "using governmental forces to affect social change" is profoundly accurate. Virtually everything the political left does or promotes involves using the force of government to change or "fix" society.

A leftist will always view society as fundamentally flawed and unfair because life isn't fair. A leftist believes that it's their divine calling to "right" the inherent "wrongs" within society. That's their ambition and purpose in life. It's what drives them. Much like the fundamentalist Christian wants every soul to be "saved," the political leftist is motivated by the constant struggle to instill their dogmatic belief of equity and fairness on society. Any political victories along their journey and within their daily fight for this sense of righteousness is what they consider as progress.

Just as the devil gets in the way of saving souls, political leftists have their own impediments to the salvation of society. Can you think of any? In staying with the fundamentalist Christian comparison (I know how much the left hate that comparison), perhaps their biggest impediment is *free will*. It's also known as freedom and liberty

There's an undeniable reason as to why the political left employs a tactic described as "social improvement through governmental action." It's because the implementation of their leftist vision of social improvement requires the force of government. It's so good, it needs to be forced upon otherwise free people against their will.

People rarely choose leftist policies. Free people rarely vote for progressive policies. If leftist policies were popular in America, progressives wouldn't need to use the force of government to impose them on American citizens. Rather, Americans would choose progressive policy freely. Isn't that elementary?

The political left has hijacked the general understanding of the term progressive, and they've done it in a most convenient way. To them, it still holds to the original definition of an adjective generally meaning the characterization of progress. That's because they're "selling" their ideas and policies as the instruments of progress for society. They're claiming that the implementation of leftist policies will work for the betterment of society.

Leftists also conflate the second definition, a noun meaning political change and social improvement by governmental action, as if the two definitions are one in the same. That's because the political left believes that they're indivisibly linked. They believe that using the power of government to force change upon society that procures their vision of equity and fairness does, indeed, represent progress.

The truth is that no matter how the political left sells progressivism, it's just another example of authoritarian government control over society. It's just another example of the left using their twisted notion of equity and fairness to erode freedom and liberty. The imposition of their sense of morality through the force of government is what they consider as progress (or as progressive). However, in truth, it's no such thing. Rather, it's another attempt to redefine the concept.

Conclusion

One of the primary purposes of clearly defining terms and concepts is to get a shared understanding of what can be complex issues that are often a point of contention in America. The act of clearly defining terms gets everyone "on the same page" so that we can move forward in debating, deliberating, and determining collectively, the best directional course for America. As with any republic, we absolutely need this level of understanding to ensure that the will of the people becomes the law of the land and remains as such.

How can we stand either for or against any concept that has a meaning that changes on the whim of a political class? How can we function within society if carefully articulated and codified laws are effectively changed by political operatives not through the proper legislative process, but simply by covertly redefining words and phrases?

"Redefining America" means taking the once commonly understood definition of a word or phrase and changing it to mean otherwise, and doing so to confuse or "game" the result primarily for political gain.

How has this been accomplished by the radical left? In part, through the redefining and ultimately the confusing and distorting of once commonly understood terms and phrases. Then, by successfully using the newly crafted meaning to manipulate the masses as well as the legal system.

Redefining is typically perpetrated by the political left through the demonization of their opposition therefore "poisoning" and shutting down any attempt at an honest and open debate. Upon successfully demonizing a political foe, what remains is simply the "good" leftist Democrats versus the successfully demonized or "evil" conservative Republicans.

This simple blueprint has resulted in the empowerment of the radical left throughout much of America. The left largely controls most of the media (sadly, even sports media), academia, federal bureaucracies, entertainment, and the "woke" companies that constitute big business in America. They also have a seemingly unbreakable level of political control over America's highly urbanized areas from coast to coast. That's quite the power base.

Has this resulted in peace, tolerance, and civility? No. America is angrier and more divided today than we've experienced in a very long time. And this is being done consciously. It's truly the politics of hate and division "packaged and sold" as the exact opposite.

It's a deceitful and ultimately destructive political strategy, but it works. The radical left doesn't concern themselves with the wreckage left behind in the wake of their scorched-earth strategy. The end justifies the means. Again, to them, it works.

The operational theory from the political left is that definitions change with a greater understanding of what these terms and phrases really mean. But is it really a greater understanding that the left is seeking? Or is it really a justification for their radical political vision? Just as the American left has purported to have "cornered the market" on caring for others in their so-called fight for righteousness, equity, peace and love, they sell their intentions as those in search of greater understanding.

Don't buy it. Don't believe it. Once people understand that the sales pitch of equity, love, peace, and righteousness is a facade hiding authoritarianism, intolerance and division for the sake of political gain and expediency, we truly begin to understand what's happening in America.

Every American should realize what "redefining" does to a representative form of government. When the American people stand collectively behind (or opposed to) a relevant concept (an issue) and vote in a manner to reflect such sentiment, what happens when the concept is redefined to mean something entirely different? It means that the will of the people is thwarted and bent to match the will of those manipulating our language.

As previously stated, a vital objective in clearly defining terms and concepts is to protect their original meaning. What good does it do for America to have a constitution as the supreme law of the land or enumerated powers, statutory law, case law or any law if radical political operatives can simply redefine the underlying terms to change fundamental meaning(s)? This redefining of basic terms and principles takes our bedrock foundation as a constitutional republic and erodes it at its core.

For example, there is only one correct way to interpret the U. S. Constitution: as originalists had intended. Redefining relevant concepts uses "new" meanings of words and phrases to make malleable the bedrock foundation of our liberty. The ultimate goal of the political left is to affect the "supreme law of the land" to mean whatever they'd like it to mean today, with the ability to conveniently change it again tomorrow if they so choose.

This is why we simply cannot allow the American left to hijack our language and redefine America. The redefining of terms such as disease, gender, violence, etc., has led to the empowerment of politicians, bureaucrats, pundits, and others legally, monetarily, morally, and otherwise. It's being done with purpose by the political left, yet "under the nose" of the rest of America. Far too many Americans are still "waking up" to a changed nation without the consent of the governed.

It's my hope that recognizing and understanding what's happening to America is only the first step towards ultimately putting an end to the political left's redefining of America.

References

"affirm." www.dictionary.com/browse/affirm. Dictionary.com 2023. Web. 9 October, 2023.

"antifa." www.dictionary.com/browse/Antifa%20. Dictionary.com 2023. Web. 10 February, 2023.

"antifa." en.wikipedia.org/wiki/Antifa Wikipedia.org 2024. Web. 10 February, 2024.

"authoritarian."www.dictionary.com/browse/ authoritarianDictionary.com 2024. Web. 19 February, 2024

"ban." www.merriam-webster.com/dictionary/ban. Merriam-Webster 2023. Web. 9 August, 2023.

Binnion, Billy. "In 2020, Words Are 'Violence,' Arson Is Not" Reason.com. 3 July, 2020.

Borgner, Matthew. The Freedom Prescription. Monee, Ill: Amazon, 2020. Print.
"Brainerd Man Sentenced To Prison, $12 million In Restitution For Minneapolis Police Third Precinct Arson."

United States Attorney's Office, District of Minnesota. 28 April, 2021. www.justice.gov/usao-mn/pr/brainerd-man-sentenced-prison-12-million-restitution-minneapolis-police-third-precinct.

Brandt, Katie Scarlett. "Healing Society's Soul." chicagohealthonline.com. 15 February, 2017.

"cancel culture." www.dictionary.com/browse/cancel-culture. Dictionary.com 2022. Web. 14 February, 2022.

Cillizza, Chris. "Donald Trump Used a Word He's 'Not Supposed To,' Here's Why." cnn.com. 23 October, 2018.

Cornell Law School, Legal Information Institute 18 U.S. Code 2383 – Rebellion or insurrection. law.cornell.edu. 15 September, 2023.

Cornell Law School, Legal Information Institute 18 U.S. Code 2384 – Seditious conspiracy. law.cornell.edu. 15 September, 2023.

"culture." www.merriam-webster.com/dictionary/culture. Merriam-Webster.com 2024. Web. 4 July, 2024.

"disease." www.merriam-webster.com/dictionary/disease. Merriam-Webster.com 2022. Web. 7 April, 2022.

"disinformation." www.merriam-webster.com/dictionary/disinformation. Merriam-Webster.com 2023. Web. 20 February, 2023.

Downey, Caroline. "Teen Girl Blasts YMCA Trans Policy after Encountering Naked Man in Women's Locker Room." yahoo.com. 17 January, 2023.

Emamzadeh, Arash. "Why People Support Far-Right Political Views." Psychologytoday.com. 6 November, 2019.

Falconer, Rebecca. "JD Vance and Tim Ryan Spar Over Racism in Heated Senate Debate." Axios.com 18 October, 2022.

"fascism." www.merriam-webster.com/dictionary/fascism. Merriam-Webster.com 2024. Web. 10 February, 2024.

"gender." www.merriam-webster.com/dictionary/gender. Merriam-Webster.com 2023 Web. 13 Feb, 2023.

Goldman, David. "What You Need To Know About The Incandescent Light Bulb Ban." cnn.com, 1 August, 2023.

"hate." www.dictionary.com/browse/hate?s=t. Dictionary.com 2020 Web. 21 February, 2020.

"illegal." www.dictionary.com/browse/illegal. Dictionary.com 2024. Web. 16 March, 2024.

"imperialism." www.merriam-webster.com/dictionary/imperialism. Merriam-Webster.com 2022. Web. 23 March, 2022.

"infrastructure." www.merriam-webster.com/dictionary/infrastructure. Merriam-Webster.com 2021. Web. 17 August, 2021.

"insurrection." www.merriam-webster.com/dictionary/insurrection. Merriam-Webster 2023. Web. 15 September, 2023.

Johnston, Isabel. "Words Matter: No Human Being is Illegal, Immigration and Human Rights Law Review." Lawblogs.uc.edu. 20 May, 2019.

Keltz, David. "Everything Is Infrastructure." spectator.org. 12 April, 2021.

Kilander, Gustaf, "'We have a moral obligation': Democrats consider using infrastructure money for Afghan refugees." independent.co.uk.com. 17 August, 2021.

Landy, Joshua. "Postmodernism: The Decline of Truth." philosophytalk.org. 15, July, 2019.

Lapin, Tamar. "'Unicorns are infrastructure': Sen. Gillibrand mocked for definition of Biden plan." nypost.com. 7 April, 2021.

Lewis, Rayna. "How the Gender Identity Revolution Impacts Society." news.temple.edu. 4 August, 2021.

"liberal." www.merriam-webster.com/dictionary/liberal. Merriam-Webster.com 2022 Web. 14 February, 2022.

Martin, Cory. "What Is the Difference Between a Disease and a Disorder?" verywellhealth.com. 9 January, 2021.

Miller, Mark Andrew. "Antifa Rioters Burn US Flags, Storm Courthouse, and Clash with Police in Portland, Oregon." washingtonexaminer.com. 12 March, 2021.

"my truth." www.urbandictionary.com/define. php?term=My%20Truth. urbandictionary.com. 2021 Web. 8 July, 2021.

"nazi." www.yourdictionary.com/nazi. yourdictionary.com. 2024. Web. 19 February, 2024.

Olsen, Tyler. "Infrastructure bill's unusual provisions: Drunk driving tech mandate to 'pollinator-friendly' roads." foxbusiness.com. 4 August, 2021.

Orso, Anna. "Oprah says, 'speak your truth.' But how is that different from 'the truth?'" inquirer.com. 10 Jan, 2018.

Ouanvilay, Mina. "'Chinese' Virus is a Racist Take – Here's Why." diversity.ncsu.edu. 3 April, 2020.

Peterson, Pia and Sadler, Hailey. "'You Want To See Your Child Grow Up:' Asylum-Seekers Sent Back To Mexico Share Their Stories." Buzzfeed News.com.
28 July, 2021.

"progressive." www.merriam-webster.com/dictionary/ progressive. Merriam-Webster.com 2024. Web. 4 March, 2024.
"race." www.merriam-webster.com/dictionary/race. Merriam-Webster.com. 2024. Web. 4 July, 2024

Rantz, Jason, "2021 Democrats Are Now Paying The Price For Empowering Antifa." nypost.com. 4 January, 2021.

Reich, Robert. "Trump and the Republican party exemplify these five elements of fascism." theguardian.com. 17 June, 2023.

"riot." www.merriam-webster.com/dictionary/riot. Merriam-Webster.com 2023. Web. 15 September, 2023.

"sexual harassment." www.merriam-webster.com/ dictionary/sexual%20harassment. Merriam-Webster.com 2022. Web. 23 Dec. 2022.

Slutkin, Gary M.D. "Violence is a Contagious Disease." National Center for Biotechnology Information, National Library of Medicine, 2010. The University of Illinois at Chicago. Copyright 2013 by the National Academy of Sciences.

https://www.ncbi.nlm.nih.gov/books/NBK207245/

Stryker, Susan. "What Does It Mean to Be a Woman? It's Complicated." time.com. 5 March, 2020.

"take care of." www.merriam-webster.com/dictionary/take%20care%20of. Merriam-Webster.com 2023. Web. 9 October, 2023.

"the far right." www.merriam-webster.com/dictionary/the%20far%20right. Merriam-Webster.com 2023. Web. 9 November, 2023.

"truth." www.dictionary.com/browse/truth. Dictionary.com 2021. Web. 8 July, 2021.

"truth." www.merriam-webster.com/dictionary/truth. Merriam-Webster.com 2021. Web. 8 July, 2021.

"undocumented." www.dictionary.com/browse/undocumented. Dictionary.com 2024. Web. 16 March, 2024.

"violence." www.merriam-webster.com/dictionary/violence. Merriam-Webster.com 2024. Web. 19 February, 2024.

"Why Do 'Left' And 'Right' Mean Liberal And Conservative?" www.dictionary.com/e/leftright/. Dictionary.com. Web. 9 November, 2023.

"woman." www.dictionary.com/browse/woman. Dictionary.com 2023. Web. 24 November, 2023.

"woman." www.merriam-webster.com/dictionary/woman.. Merriam-Webster.com 2023. Web. 24 November, 2023.

Yuko, Elizabeth. "What Is Book Banning, and How Does It Affect Society." rd.com. 15 February, 2023.

About the Author

Matthew R. Borgner completed his undergraduate coursework at The Ohio State University and earned a Master's in Political Science from the University of Akron. Along with *Redefining America,* he is the author of *The Freedom Prescription.* His working background includes over a quarter century of service for the great state of Ohio. He is a Canton, Ohio, native, where he resides with his wife and son.

www.ingramcontent.com/pod-product-compliance
Lightning Source LLC
Chambersburg PA
CBHW060621130626
46555CB00002B/602